Nailed It!

INTRODUCTION BY

JACQUES TORRES

BAKING CHALLENGES
FOR THE REST OF US

Nailed It!

BY THE CREATORS OF *Nailed It!*

WITH HEATHER MACLEAN

ABRAMS IMAGE, NEW YORK

CONTENTS

Bonjour!

from **JACQUES TORRES**

Welcome to the official *Nailed It!* cookbook! Whether you are an experienced baker looking to challenge yourself or have never baked without a cake mix, I am so very glad you have chosen to come on this baking journey with us.

I think what makes the show so authentically delightful is that it proves that everyone can bake and have a good time doing it. We rarely get anything perfect on the first try. Do you remember the first day you rode a bicycle? You fell! Nobody jumps on a bicycle and doesn't fall. But you get back up, learn from your experience, and try again. And eventually, you get better until you're riding around as if you were born doing it.

It's the same with baking. Everyone starts out less-than-perfect and if you make sure to have fun while you're doing it, you cannot lose. I tell the new chefs in my kitchen: You might not do it as well as me the first time, but do it a couple times and you'll improve, and eventually you might even do it better than me!

I know the kitchen can be an intimidating place for many people, but it shouldn't be! It is actually the best place to spend time with your friends and family—to cook and be together. My son is four years old, so everything he touches in the kitchen is a little bit of a catastrophe, but he loves trying and discovering. He really enjoys making and decorating cookies and chocolates. Even when I make my coffee in the morning, he says, "Papa, let me do it for you!"

How cute is that? My daughter is two, and when we made gingerbread houses this holiday season, she put more of the candy in her mouth than on the house. It's fun to crack eggs, play with dough, decorate with frosting and mold chocolate.

My favorite part of *Nailed It!* and this book is that they show us things don't have to be perfect to be wonderful. Too often, the stress of modern life causes us to want everything to be a certain way. You might end up with a cake that's a little bit crooked or doesn't look exactly right, but you will still have a cake! A *delicious* one, as long as you promise to read the recipe and not swap the sugar for salt or something (my mouth still tingles at the memory of that Humpty Dumpty cupcake from Season 2). No matter how your recipes turn out, you should be proud of yourself too. Proud that you tried something so outrageous (like an erupting volcano cake!), that you opened yourself up to a new experience, and that you learned along the way.

I am proud of you for challenging yourself with these crazy recipes and cannot wait to see the amazing creations you make. I am rooting for you, and I know that in the end, you will have nailed it!

Happy Baking!
Jacques

Share your creations with me on social media @jacquestorres using #NailedItCookbook

Baking used to be nothing but joy. Sweet, sweet joy.

A stress-relieving activity for family and friends that started in giggles and ended in something delicious. Enter Pinterest and Photoshop. Like the horsemen of the Apocalypse, they rode in and destroyed the dream. Suddenly, our feeds were filled with images of dessert perfection, and we were stuffed with shame.

The gorgeous photographs called to us, and we wanted to make it all: the rubber ducky cupcakes, the rock candy geode cakes, the elaborately braided pies, the ombré mermaid milkshakes. The pictures made it look so easy. But it was all a lie.

We should've guessed from the number of rainbow unicorns that the photos were selling a fantasy, but we tried anyway. And failed. Oh, how we failed! Our colors bled, our cakes collapsed, and our mythical horses looked like monsters. Frustration built, tears were shed, and more than one birthday was ruined.

Our only solace was in seeing the fails of others posted online—but laughing at someone else's melted Cookie Monster didn't make up for our wasted time and trash can food.

Then, we had an idea. What if we celebrated our failures instead of crying over them? What if we invited everyone else who'd failed to laugh with us? And so, *Nailed It!* was born. *Nailed It!* was never about trying to find the worst of the worst; it was about the best of the rest of us. Because regular baking isn't supposed to be diabolically hard. We're not losers if we can't temper chocolate (or we don't even know what made the chocolate angry in the first place)—we're winners because we tried.

The instant success of the show around the world proved we weren't the only ones craving a more realistic approach to dessert making. We discovered pretty quickly that once you take away the pressure of perfection, baking goes back to being fun, even—and maybe especially—when we fail.

At its core, *Nailed It!* is about the joy of the process. Because let's be honest, doing anything with tons of butter and sugar and sprinkles is a good time. And whether you build a wedding cake worthy of Sylvia Weinstock or the Leaning Tower of Pastry, because of all that butter and sugar and sprinkles, the end result is going to taste amazing.

With the official *Nailed It!* cookbook, we're bringing the party to you. We've collected our best recipes, behind-the-scenes stories, and actually helpful tips from our resident experts so you can become a master baker from the comfort of your own kitchen. Or not. The goal isn't excellence, it's enjoyment. We'll give you all the instruction you need to whip up some truly wild creations. It doesn't matter whether they turn out insanely beautiful or just insane. Either way, you can be proud that you nailed it!

Get yourself a golden baker's cap, grab your kids or your bestie, and get your bake on!

Book Ingredients

WORK IT!

Quick tutorials on some basic baking building blocks, like how to shape rice cereal and work with fondant so you don't read a recipe and go, "Whaaat?"

BAKER'S CHOICE

Just like on the show, these are quicker, less-involved recipes. Here's where you'll find cake pops, cupcakes, donuts, and smaller cakes including a few designed specifically to be made at home—perfect for kids, first-timers, friendly competitions, and quick(ish) bakes.

NAIL IT OR FAIL IT

These are the quintessential cake recipes that put your skills to the test. Get ready for castles, mountains, volcanoes, airplanes, piñatas, and, yes, even a unicorn. These recipes are intended to be true challenges and involve more time and ingredients than those behind Door #1, but fear not: We will equip you with detailed instructions and plenty of Frosted Tips to help you in your attempt!

NAILED IT! HOLIDAY!

Special holiday desserts to help you celebrate the season. Deck the halls with boughs of holy moly and ho-ho-oh-no!

DONUT YOU DARE

A choose-your-own-recipe adventure for making delightful critter-shaped donuts. Options range from making each component from scratch (including deep-frying in oil!) to buying donuts from the store and simply decorating them, as well as everything in between.

HOW TO HOST A *NAILED IT!* PARTY

Everything you need to know to throw your own *Nailed It!* themed party, whether you're celebrating a kid's birthday or you just want to see adults cry (with laughter!).

FROSTED TIP

Want to know how professionals cut costs on ingredients? They buy in bulk. Your friendly neighborhood warehouse club is a great place to find fifteen-pound bags of sugar for $5. Our best buy (especially since buttercream covers all sins): jumbo bags of powdered sugar. A seven-pound bag costs around $4 and holds about twenty-six cups of sugar.

JACQUES' ATTACK

My Best Advice for Beginners

1. Read the Recipe First

Before you begin, read the entire recipe through. That way you'll know what you're getting into and you won't be surprised by a step you aren't prepared for.

2. Gather Everything You'll Need in One Place

Before I start anything in the kitchen, I make sure everything I will need is laid out on the table: the recipe, the ingredients, and the tools. In France, we call this *mise en place* (mee-zan-PLAHS), or "everything in its place." Doing this will save you time and heartbreak later so you won't get to step 3 and realize you are missing something important. It also makes the entire process much easier.

3. Stop and Take Five

I always say this on the show: Stop for five minutes and make a plan. When things are not going the way you'd hoped, instead of wasting more time, just stop and take a step back. Look over what you are doing. Take a deep breath. And smile! Ironically, these five minutes to reset and make a new plan will save so much time . . . and possibly your recipe.

4. Add Your Favorite Flavors

New bakers are always afraid to deviate from the recipe, but when it comes to adding flavor, don't be! Maybe the recipe doesn't include cranberry or chocolate, but if your gut tells you it's going to be good, add it! I like a surprise when I eat a cake; I hate a bland cake. Don't be afraid to add extra flavors that you love: vanilla, coffee, strawberry, raisins, nuts, whatever you want.

5. Don't Give Up!

No matter how they turn out, you should be proud of your creations. You tried something so outrageous, like a robot cake with glowing eyes, and opened yourself up to a new experience. If you didn't nail it this time, you will the next!

Five Questions

—WITH HEAD JUDGE—

JACQUES TORRES

How did you first learn about *Nailed It!*?

I was contacted by the producers to be the head judge of a new reality baking competition show that was about people trying their best with humor and heart even if—or more likely, when—their cake fell apart. It wasn't about winning or losing, it was about trying something new. Pushing yourself to make something delicious, learning from your mistakes, and eventually trying again. It would be full of laughter, and they assured me there would be no tears or mean exchanges. I thought this was something I would love to be part of. Creating pastry and teaching the art of pastry are my two passions! In addition to my career as a pastry chef and chocolatier, I was simultaneously the Dean of Pastry for about thirty years at the International Culinary Institute in New York. *Nailed It!* really is my ultimate playground and ties in all my personal joys in one place. I laugh with Nicole, guest judges, and contestants; I teach about pastry; and every now and then they let me make and demonstrate recipes. I hope you can see my joy through your screens.

Had you met Nicole Byer before the show?

I had the pleasure of meeting Nicole on set taping our very first episode. I had known I was going to be lucky to work with a professional comedian, but that first twelve-hour day of shooting, she truly surprised me with her immense talent. Not only did she have me and the entire 100+ person crew laughing hysterically, but she also is a true professional and extremely kind and a good person. What a wonderful surprise that we would become such good friends when we are so different. Nicole is the complete opposite of me in many ways.

I'm French, she's American. I'm a chef, she doesn't cook. But we work so well together and really click. She is full of love, energy, and joyous laughter. Nicole is a treasure!

Has any contestant ever quit during a challenge?

Nicole and I work very hard to make sure no one gives up. We do whatever it takes to support them. It's not easy to come on television and try something you are not already good at. Our contestants are very brave! I give them a lot of credit. Plus, they are so funny! Everyone has just been delightful. So, to answer this question: No one has quit a challenge.

You're known as Mr. Chocolate. Does everyone in your house have a nickname?

Yes, actually. My wife, who is also a chocolatier, is known as Madame Chocolat. My son, I call him My Little Bonbon. And my daughter is My Little Truffle.

What is the secret to great buttercream?

Ah, this is a question I love! To start, it is a lot easier to make a good buttercream if you have a stand mixer. And here is the secret that professionals know: Don't use the mixer on full speed. Sometimes we think the faster we beat something, the more volume it will have. It doesn't work like that with buttercream, though, because it's an *emulsion*—Nicole always makes fun of that word—a combination of two liquids that don't want to be mixed, like oil and water. Mixing on the highest speed does not help the process; it hurts it and can make your buttercream less sweet! Also, if your buttercream becomes a little too soft, put it in the fridge for fifteen minutes and then mix it again.

WORK IT!

Tips for Working with Our Favorite Ingredients

You know that coworker who doesn't always do what they're supposed to? (Wes.) Or that elusive person you've always heard about but never met? (Wes's beautiful wife.) Some baking components are like that. Here's what you need to know to get the best out of them.

Modeling Chocolate

Also called sculpting chocolate, modeling chocolate—basically just chocolate mixed with corn syrup—is a lot like clay, except you can eat it. It's soft and malleable, making it perfect for shaping figures and adding details to desserts. It's not as stretchy as fondant, and it dries harder, so modeling chocolate is usually just used for accessorizing, rather than covering entire cakes. You can buy it in tubs online or at craft and specialty stores or make it yourself.

Coloring It: You can turn white modeling chocolate into any color you want using gel or liquid food coloring. Add a drop or two and knead away. Just don't forget to wear food-safe gloves; otherwise, your hands will look funky *for days.*

Working with It: Exactly like with clay, you break off little bits, knead them until they're soft, and form them into anything you wish. To roll it flat and cut out shapes, use either a nonstick fondant rolling pin and a silicone mat, or a regular rolling pin and any surface lightly dusted with powdered sugar or cornstarch. You can also use little tools to twist and cut and mark patterns on modeling chocolate—just make sure they're food-safe.

Hot Tip: It is chocolate and it will melt in your hot hands, so try not to overhandle it, and work with small pieces at a time. You can also stick your hands in ice water first to cool them down (make sure they're completely dry afterward), crank up the air conditioning, or stick the chocolate in the refrigerator for a few minutes if you find it's melting. A light dusting of cornstarch can also keep it from sticking to your hands.

Fondant

Fondant is like a curtain made out of icing. If you want to cover a cake, especially one stacked and cut into different shapes, with a single, smooth coating that holds everything together, fondant is your jam. It's sold premade in packets or tubs online and at craft and specialty stores. Depending on what kind you buy and how old it is, you may have to knead it to soften it before you can shape it. Fondant is made from sugar, fat, water, and gelatin, so it's very pliable, and, of course, edible, but to be honest, it doesn't taste all that great by itself.

Coloring It: Fondant is sold in a range of colors, but you can also color it yourself with gel or liquid food coloring. Just add a drop or two and knead the color throughout. We highly recommend wearing food-safe gloves when you do, unless you want to look like you strangled a

Smurf, a leprechaun, or Elmo—for a week.

Working with It: Fondant is like a cross between clay and dough. You generally start by kneading a chunk until it's pliable, then rolling it out flat with either a nonstick fondant rolling pin and a silicone mat, or a regular rolling pin and any surface lightly dusted with powdered sugar or cornstarch. Don't roll it too thin, however, or it might break. Fondant is very forgiving and can be slightly stretched and tucked and molded around almost any cake or rice cereal shape.

Hot Tip: Fondant will start to harden as soon as you open it, so don't dawdle. You can repair tears or cracks with patches of fondant and your fingers dipped in vegetable oil to smooth the new piece over the old Before you stick anything three-dimensional—like a flamingo neck or pilot dude—onto a dessert, you'll want to let your formed creation rest on a flat surface so it *can* harden a bit. If you stick it on your cake right away, it might droop, which would just be sad for everyone.

Royal Icing

That smooth, hard, shiny icing that decorates the fancy cookies in the bakery? It's called royal icing. Nobody really knows why, but it was slathered all over Queen Victoria and Prince Albert's wedding cake back in 1840, so there's that. Even though it hardens like a candy glaze, it's very edible and very delicious.

Working with It: The icing starts very runny and can be used as a dip, with a spoon, or in a piping bag. If your goal is to cover a surface, pipe an outline, then fill the middle in afterward. You can control how thick or thin you want your icing to be, depending on what you need it to do, by adding a little bit of powdered sugar (to thicken it) or water (to thin it).

Coloring It: Just a drop or two of gel or liquid food coloring stirred in will turn your royal icing into a colorful treat. It will darken a bit as it dries.

Hot Tip: Stir your icing frequently to prevent it from hardening before you're done using it. If it does start to get crusty, add a couple of drops of water to soften it again. Don't go poking your fingers onto your beautiful creations after you've decorated them, or else you'll get fingerprints all over them, since royal icing takes six to eight hours to harden completely.

Rice Cereal Shapes

Most of us know rice cereal squares as a stand-alone dessert, but for professional cake decorators, they're a secret building block stuffed into the middle of towering creations to give a solid, still-edible foundation.

To Create Large Sculptures: Make the mixture as you would for squares. Line a pan with parchment paper or cellophane wrap lightly sprayed with vegetable oil. Spread a little oil or shortening onto the palms of your hands and then smash the cereal and marshmallow goodness down into the pan as far as you can. The denser it is, the stronger it will be. Refrigerate it until firm. Once it's nice and solid, remove your rice cereal sheet from the pan, and cut it into whatever shapes you'd like. To build a large structure, you can "glue" bricks together with melted chocolate. Once stacked, use a serrated knife to carve the block into whatever shape you desire.

To Create Smaller Hand-Molded Shapes: Make the mixture as you would for squares, but leave it in the bowl for ten minutes to cool. Spread a little oil or shortening onto the palms of your hands and then grab handfuls of the mixture and squoosh them as you see fit. The harder you squish your shapes, the stronger they'll be. Once hardened, they can also be carved with a small, serrated knife.

FOOD COLORING TIP

While powder, paste, or liquid food coloring will work, we find gel food coloring gives the most vibrant results. You can find gel food coloring online or at craft stores.

Buttercream Basics

Like Jacques, we're big fans of butt-ARR-cream!, but the silky frosting can be made many different ways. Swiss and Italian meringue buttercream use egg whites, French buttercream incorporates egg yolks, and German buttercream is custard-based.

Nailed It! creations use a standard American buttercream recipe with just five ingredients—butter, powdered sugar, milk, vanilla, and salt—because it's uncomplicated, firm enough for decorating, easily colored, and tastes delicious. But nothing is entirely foolproof, so we have a few buttercream tips for you to keep in mind:

• Your butter must be room temperature. Not cold from the fridge, not squishy in places from the microwave, just plain old room temperature. To achieve this, take butter out of the fridge at least 20 minutes before you start making your buttercream. To speed things up, you can cut the butter into chunks first (a step we recommend in our recipes anyway to keep the butter from blobbing all over your mixer).

• If your buttercream starts to get too soft after it's made, stick it in the fridge for 10 minutes to firm it up again.

• If you feel that your buttercream is too soft overall, add more powdered sugar 1 table-spoon at a time until it reaches a thickness you like.

• If you feel that your buttercream is too firm, add more milk 1 tablespoon at a time until it reaches a thickness you like.

• You can substitute either heavy cream or skim milk for the whole milk in our buttercream recipe, but keep in mind that it will slightly change the consistency. Heavy cream will make for stiffer buttercream; milk with less fat will make for softer buttercream. You can adjust for this by using more or less milk or adding more powdered sugar (again, just a tablespoon at a time).

• Your buttercream might be the perfect consistency for spreading around the outside of a cake but a little too soft for piping the perfect unicorn mane. To stiffen it up before putting it into a piping bag, add a couple of tablespoons of powdered sugar.

Extra Buttercream

The perfect ratio of buttercream to cake is a highly personal decision. Some people like a nice, modest layer; others want their tastebuds swimming in creamy goodness. While we tried to give you enough buttercream for every recipe, if you ever want more, here is the recipe for whipping up a few different quantities:

1 Cup Buttercream

¼ cup (½ stick/56 g) unsalted butter, room temperature, cut into chunks

1 cup (125 g) powdered sugar

½ teaspoon vanilla extract

Pinch of salt

1½ teaspoons (7 ml) whole milk

2 Cups Buttercream

½ cup (1 stick/112 g) unsalted butter, room temperature, cut into chunks

2 cups (250 g) powdered sugar

1 teaspoon vanilla extract

Pinch of salt

1 tablespoon (15 ml) whole milk

4 Cups Buttercream

1 cup (2 sticks/225 g) unsalted butter, room temperature, cut into chunks

4 cups (500 g) powdered sugar

2 teaspoons vanilla extract

⅛ teaspoon salt

2 tablespoons (30 ml) whole milk

1. Using a mixer, beat the butter until creamy, about 1 minute.

2. Add powdered sugar one cup (125 g) at a time, mixing until well combined.

3. Add vanilla, salt, and milk, and mix on high until thick and creamy. If the buttercream is too thin, add more powdered sugar, 1 tablespoon at a time. If the buttercream is too thick, add more milk, 1 tablespoon at a time.

How to Make a
GOLDEN BAKER'S CAP

Anyone who signs up to find the fun in failure is a winner in our book. Go ahead and make yourself the baker's cap you deserve.

Materials Needed

- 1 8½ by 11-inch (216 by 279-mm) or A4 sheet white card stock
- 2 sheets gold glitter tissue paper
- Scotch tape

Instructions

1. Cut the card stock lengthwise into two strips, each 3 inches (7.5 cm) wide. Tape the strips together at the ends to form one long strip. Wrap the strip around the baker's head to determine the proper circumference, and trim the excess, leaving 2 inches (5 cm) for overlap.

2. Cut one sheet of tissue paper into lengthwise strips 5 inches (12.5 cm) wide each.

3. Lay the card stock strip flat on top of a tissue paper strip, centering the card stock down the length of the tissue paper strip. Fold the tissue paper edges around the card stock, and secure with tape. Repeat if needed until the card stock strip is covered in gold tissue paper on one side.

4. Take the uncut second sheet of tissue paper and begin taping the bottom edge inside the top edge of the card stock strip, securing it to the back, uncovered side of the card stock strip. Bunch the tissue paper into messy folds as you go to create the pleats and folds that will give the hat's top some volume. Continue until you reach the end of the tissue paper, so one straight edge of the tissue paper is completely secured to the card stock.

5. Tape the ends of the card stock strip together with the overlap to make the hat's brim.

6. Take the loose top edge of the tissue paper and fold it over, creating a puffed top for the hat. Secure it to the inside of the brim opposite the taped-down bottom edge, again bunching it into folds as you go, and tape it to the inside of the brim.

7. Carefully repeat with the two untaped edges of the tissue paper top, folding them down into the circle and taping them into bunches.

8. Puff the tissue paper up from the inside and wear it with pride!

Our first-ever guest judge, known as the "Queen of Cakes" because of her celebrated wedding cakes, began her career as a teacher and didn't start professionally baking until she was fifty! Her very first cake was just two layers; her largest so far was ten feet tall.

SYLVIA WEINSTOCK

▶ **What was the best part about being on *Nailed It!*?**

I just love being with Jacques Torres and Nicole Byer. And I loved the enthusiasm and the commitment of the bakers. They were perfectly willing to accept failure. They took the challenges in stride and had such good attitudes. That's the most important thing: attitude. If your attitude is to do your very best, you will.

▶ **What has the fan reaction been like?**

It's just been incredible. I get letters from all over the United States and around the world—Germany, Slovakia, South America. A lot of letters come from young people saying that they want to be artists, that they love the idea of creating something. And baking is art!

▶ **In the very first episode, you joked about keeping one of the pans from the set. Did you?**

No, but the production was really lovely and sent it to me afterward as a gift. It's really such a good pan because it's so smooth inside. The rivets are on the outside, not the inside like most pans. When you have rivets on the inside, you need a toothpick to clean them out.

▶ **Did you learn anything from the contestants?**

I learned courage. They were extraordinary, gutsy people. It takes guts to try to imitate professional work in a short timeframe with unfamiliar ingredients and recipes and tools.

▶ **What's your favorite dessert?**

A simple yeast coffee cake. I'm not into things that are too sweet. My favorite flavor is lemon.

▶ **How can you fix a cake that fell apart or looks terrible?**

Easy! Cut it up and make what the English call a trifle. Get a glass bowl and layer pieces with whatever fillings you like—jams, creams, fruit, and nuts. Gorgeous and delicious.

▶ **Any advice for home bakers?**

Aim for the best. That's my credo in business and in life. If you want to make something that's delicious, you must use the best ingredients. You can tell when someone isn't using great ingredients. If you want to make the best-tasting dessert, get the most expensive butter and heavy cream, the freshest fruit and freshest eggs you can find.

WESSSSS!!!

It's
WESTON BAHR

While he's game for almost anything on set—from dressing like Thor to transforming into a human New Year's countdown (disco) ball—Wes isn't a comedic plant, he's actually the show's very talented, extremely busy associate director. We got the happily married father of one to answer a few quick questions.

▶ **Can you bake?**

Not as well as I can cook, but I can hold my own.

▶ **Who taught you?**

My mom.

▶ **What's your best dish?**

My mom's apple pie.

▶ **What's your favorite dessert to eat?**

My mom's apple pie.

▶ **What is your favorite moment from the show?**

During the first season when we were figuring out how I would come out with the *Nailed It!* trophy. It was never a scripted beat, so it would just be the camera operators and me coming up with stuff on the fly.

▶ **Any advice for young viewers?**

Pursue what you're passionate about with reckless abandon. You might not figure out what it is right away, but once you have, put your heart into it and there is nothing you can't do.

SMALLER, EASY-ISH RECIPES *to get your* CULINARY JUICES FLOWING

BAKER'S CHOICE

CHOCOLATE EMOJI CAKE

Season 1, Episode 5, "Big in Japan"

Makes one 2-layer, 6-inch (15-cm) cake

Is there anything easier than a straight-up circle cake? Is there anything cuter than a happy, yellow emoji cake? Nope and nope. We're giving you a Baker's Choice to pick your favorite emoji for this, the easiest dessert ever featured on the show: a two-layer chocolate cake with vanilla buttercream designed by cake artist Yolanda Gampp.

FOR THE CAKE

1 cup (125 g) all-purpose flour

¼ cup (25 g) unsweetened cocoa

1 teaspoon baking powder

½ teaspoon baking soda

⅛ teaspoon salt

2 large eggs

1 cup (200 g) sugar

⅓ cup (75 g) unsalted butter, room temperature, cut in chunks

½ teaspoon vanilla extract

½ cup (120 ml) whole milk

FOR THE BUTTERCREAM

1 cup (2 sticks/225 g) unsalted butter, softened

4 cups (500 g) powdered sugar

2 teaspoons vanilla extract

⅛ teaspoon salt

2 tablespoons (30 ml) whole milk

FOR THE DECORATIONS

Cornstarch

8 ounces (225 g) yellow fondant

4 ounces (115 g) black fondant

2 ounces (55 g) red, blue, or white fondant, as needed

SPECIAL EQUIPMENT

Two 6-inch (15-cm) round cake pans

Make the Cake

1. Preheat the oven to 325°F (165°C). Grease the pans. (Please learn from one of the most common mistakes on *Nailed It!* and remember to ALWAYS. GREASE. YOUR. PANS!) Cut out two 6-inch (15-cm) circles of parchment paper and place in the bottom of each pan.

2. In a medium bowl, sift together the flour, cocoa, baking powder, baking soda, and salt.

3. In a large bowl, using an electric mixer, combine the eggs, sugar, butter, vanilla, and milk. Add the dry mixture a large spoonful at a time and mix until just combined. Do not overmix. Use a spatula to scrape the sides and bottom of the bowl to incorporate the last bits of dry ingredients.

4. Pour the batter into the pans, filling halfway. Bake for 24 to 28 minutes, until a toothpick inserted in the center comes out clean. Let cool in the pans.

Make the Buttercream

1. In a large bowl, using an electric mixer, beat the butter until creamy, about 1 minute.

2. Add the powdered sugar 1 cup (125 g) at a time, mixing until well combined.

3. Add the vanilla, salt, and milk, and mix on high (but not "splatter your whole kitchen" high—unless that's the look you're going for) until thick and creamy. If the buttercream is too thin, add more powdered sugar, 1 tablespoon at a time. If the buttercream is too thick, add more milk, 1 tablespoon at a time.

Assemble the Cake

1. Run a butter knife around the edge of the cake pans. Place a plate over the pan and flip. Tap the bottom until the cake slips out. (If it does, congratulations! You're already ahead of the game.) Remove the parchment paper. Repeat for the second cake. If a cake has a domed top, flip it over and cut it off with a large, serrated knife so the top is level.

2. With a spatula (an offset spatula works great if you have one), spread a layer of buttercream about ¼ to ½ inch (7 to 12 mm) thick on top of one cake. Place the other cake on top; press gently. Spread the remaining buttercream over the entire cake.

Decorate!

1. Lightly dust a flat surface with cornstarch. Roll out the yellow fondant into a circle about 12 inches (30.5 cm) wide. Lay the fondant over the cake and smooth it down with your hands. Trim any excess from around the bottom.

2. Dust the flat surface with cornstarch again, if necessary, and roll out the black fondant. Cut out the shapes you desire. Use drops of water to "glue" the fondant decorations into place. Add a red heart or blue tears, if your cake is feeling flirty or crying with laughter (or both—we don't judge).

FROSTED TIP

Fill cake pans only halfway unless you want the batter to spill over and cook on the bottom of the oven. Have extra batter? Save it to make a few cupcakes!

SHEEP CAKE POPS

Nailed It! Holiday! Season 1. Episode 1. "Jingle Fails"

Makes about 24 cake pops

We're going to let you off easy, with just one of the cake pops from the Nativity scene that originally included three wise men, three barnyard animals, and the holy family themselves. Once you've mastered this adorable sheep, feel free to decorate the rest of the set.

FOR THE CAKE

1¼ cups (155 g) all-purpose flour

1 teaspoon baking powder

½ teaspoon baking soda

⅛ teaspoon salt

2 large eggs

1 cup (200 g) sugar

⅓ cup (75 g) unsalted butter, melted

½ teaspoon vanilla extract

½ cup (120 ml) whole milk

FOR THE BUTTERCREAM

1 cup (2 sticks/225 g) unsalted butter, softened

4 cups (500 g) powdered sugar

2 teaspoons vanilla extract

⅛ teaspoon salt

¼ cup (60 ml) whole milk

FOR THE DECORATIONS

1 bag (14 to 16 ounces/400 to 455 g) white candy melts

8 ounces (225 g) white fondant

Black food coloring

Cornstarch

SPECIAL EQUIPMENT

9 by 13-inch (23 by 33-cm) baking pan

24 paper lollipop sticks

Foam block or cake pop stand

Small food-safe paintbrush

Make the Cake

1. Preheat the oven to 350°F (175°C). Grease the baking pan.

2. In a medium bowl, sift together the flour, baking powder, baking soda, and salt.

3. In a large bowl, using an electric mixer, combine the eggs, sugar, butter, vanilla, and milk. Add the dry mixture a spoonful at a time and mix until just combined. Do not overmix. Use a spatula to scrape the sides and bottom of the bowl to incorporate the last bits of dry ingredients.

4. Pour the batter into the pan, filling halfway. (You read our tip on page 27, right? That's HALFWAY.) Bake for 16 to 18 minutes, until pale golden brown or a toothpick inserted in the center comes out clean. Let cool.

Make the Buttercream

1. In a large bowl, using an electric mixer, beat the butter until creamy, about 1 minute.

2. Add the powdered sugar 1 cup (125 g) at a time, mixing until well combined.

3. Add the vanilla, salt, and milk, and mix on high until thick and creamy. If the buttercream is too thin, add more powdered sugar, 1 tablespoon at a time. If the buttercream is too thick, add more milk, 1 tablespoon at a time.

Assemble the Cake Pops

1. Put a piece of parchment paper on a plate, and make sure there's room for it in your freezer. (Trust us; it's better to figure this out now than when you've got cake mush hands.)

2. Once the cake is cool to the touch, scoop it out of the pan and into a large bowl. Add the buttercream a generous scoop at a time and knead the whole mess with your hands until you have a nice, not-too-sticky consistency that will hold a spherical shape without crumbling.

3. Shape spheres about the size of golf balls and place on the plate. Freeze for at least 15 minutes.

Decorate!

1. Place the candy melts in a microwave-safe glass bowl. Microwave in 10-second bursts, stirring after each, until smooth. Remove the cake balls from the freezer. Dip 1 inch (2.5 cm) of a lollipop stick into the melted candy and insert it into one cake ball. Repeat with all cake balls, then return them to freezer for 5 minutes.

2. Stir the candy, and re-melt in the microwave if necessary. Working with a few cake pops at a time, remove some from the freezer. Submerge a cake pop halfway into the melted candy—not all the way in, or the ball might fall off its stick. With the cake pop half in the candy, use a spoon to coat the remainder of the cake ball with candy melt. Remove the cake pop from the candy and shake gently to remove any excess. Stick the cake pop into the foam block or cake pop stand to set until firm. Repeat with the remaining pops. When all are coated, set the candy melt bowl aside—do *not* wash it or get it wet! We need to use it again in a minute.

3. Break off a quarter of the fondant and set aside. Zap the melted candy melts in the microwave for 10-second bursts until soft again.

4. Pull off pieces of the fondant and roll them into 2-inch (5-cm) spaghetti-like strands. Curl the strands into spirals. Dip your paintbrush into the melted candy, place a dot onto a cake pop, and "glue" a curl into place. Repeat until the cake pop is covered with spirals.

5. Take the white fondant you set aside and dye it black. Dust a flat surface with cornstarch, then roll out the fondant and cut out a sheep face. "Glue" it onto the cake pop with melted candy as before. Add eyes and more curls to face. Repeat for the rest of the cake pops.

3, 2, 1 . . . Ya' done!

FROSTED TIP

Avoid adding unexpected crunch to your cake by cracking eggs on a flat surface instead of the edge of your bowl.

ALIEN CUPCAKES

Season 2, Episode 6, "Out of This World"

Makes 2 double-stacked alien cupcakes and 8–10+ regular cupcakes

These extraterrestrial treats flew from the show straight to viewers' kitchens via the *Nailed It! At Home Experience*. Netflix and a company called Fever produced these virtual events where *Nailed It!* fans attempted recipes that were brought to life by Red Velvet NYC, a company that creates DIY baking kits.

PANIC

DON'T HAVE A MUFFIN PAN

If you don't have a muffin pan, you can place the cupcake liners in oven-safe mugs.

FOR THE CUPCAKES

1½ cups (190 g) all-purpose flour

½ teaspoon baking powder

½ teaspoon baking soda

½ teaspoon salt

2 large eggs

⅔ cup (135 g) sugar

½ cup (120 ml) vegetable oil

1 teaspoon vanilla extract

⅔ cup (165 ml) whole milk

FOR THE BUTTERCREAM

1 cup (2 sticks/225 g) unsalted butter, softened

4 cups (500 g) powdered sugar

2 teaspoons vanilla extract

⅛ teaspoon salt

2 tablespoons (30 ml) whole milk

FOR THE DECORATIONS

4 ounces (115 g) white fondant

Yellow, green, and black food coloring

6 large marshmallows

12 mini marshmallows

SPECIAL EQUIPMENT

12-cup cupcake pan

Purple cupcake liners

14 wooden skewers

Cake decorating wire or paperclips

Make the Cupcakes

1. Preheat the oven to 350°F (175°C). Place the purple liners inside the pan.

2. In a medium bowl, sift together the flour, baking powder, baking soda, and salt. Set aside.

3. In a medium bowl, using an electric mixer, beat the eggs on high speed for 1 minute. Add the sugar and beat for 5 minutes. Add the vegetable oil and vanilla and mix until the batter is smooth, about 1 minute. Reduce the speed to low and alternate adding the flour mixture and the milk, beating until just combined.

4. Fill the cupcake liners halfway (we want flat, not domed, tops). Bake for 15 to 20 minutes, until the tops are pale golden brown and a toothpick inserted into the center comes out clean. Let cool.

Make the Buttercream

1. In a large bowl, using an electric mixer, beat the butter until creamy, about 1 minute.

2. Add the powdered sugar 1 cup (125 g) at a time, mixing until well combined.

3. Add the vanilla, salt, and milk, and mix on high until thick and creamy. If the buttercream is too thin, add more powdered sugar, 1 tablespoon at a time. If the buttercream is too thick, add more milk, 1 tablespoon at a time.

4. Use green food coloring to dye the buttercream.

Assemble the Aliens

1. Cut four skewers 3 inches (7.5 cm) long.

2. Grab two cooled cupcakes. Make sure they both have flat tops; if they don't, use a serrated knife to cut off any excess. (Bonus if that happens: You just found yourself a snack!) Spread a layer of buttercream on top of one cupcake and stick two skewers 1 inch (2 cm) apart in the middle of it. Take the cupcake liner off the other cupcake, turn it upside down, and stick it onto the skewers so you have two cupcakes stacked face to face, "glued" together by buttercream. Repeat with two more cupcakes.

3. Use a spatula to spread a layer of buttercream onto each cupcake stack. Add 2 tablespoons of powdered sugar to the remaining buttercream and stir to stiffen it. Place the buttercream in a plastic piping bag, snip off one end, and pipe on long, shaggy alien hair.

Decorate!

1. Pull off two small balls of fondant, each about 1 inch (2.5 cm) in diameter, and color one yellow and one black. Color the remaining fondant green.

2. Using fondant, make 12 thick green tentacles built around wooden skewers cut to around 3 inches (7.5 cm) in length, leaving about 1 inch (2.5 cm) of skewer exposed. Attach 6 tentacles to the sides of each cupcake by pressing the exposed ends of the skewers into the cake.

3. Roll the yellow fondant flat until it's about ¼ inch (6 mm) thick and cut out 12 triangular alien teeth. Roll the rest of the yellow fondant into thin ropes and decorate the green tentacles with circular "suckers."

4. Roll out the black fondant to about ¼ inch (6 mm) thick. Cut out 2 noses and mouths. Attach the mouths, teeth, and noses using a tiny bit of water to "glue" them into place. For the black eyes, dip the end of a skewer in black food coloring and dot the marshmallows.

5. Place the marshmallows on cake wire or clean paperclips and stick 3 large and 6 small all over each cupcake.

6. Frost the tops of the remaining cupcakes with buttercream and place them around the aliens.

3, 2, 1 . . . Ya' done!

FROSTED TIP

Don't overwork the fondant or it will get sticky. If that happens, sprinkle it with a pinch of cornstarch.

CANDY APPLE ALIENS

Season 6, Episode 2, "Paranormal Pastries"

Makes 1 candy apple

We can't seem to quit aliens, perhaps because they offer so much color and creativity! (Hopefully not for any other reason . . . like alien mind control.) This is another Baker's Choice where you can pick which color apple you'd like to make—or make all three!

FOR THE APPLES

1 Granny Smith apple, stem removed if necessary

25 single-colored Jolly Rancher candies— blue, red, or green

Edible glitter

4 ounces (115 g) white fondant

Food coloring to match the candies—blue, red, or green

SPECIAL EQUIPMENT

One 5-inch (12-cm), pointed, wooden lollipop stick

Toothpicks

Melt the Candy

1. Line a plate with wax paper. Stick the skewer firmly into the top of the apple.

2. Take the candies out of their wrappers and place them in a medium microwave-safe bowl. Microwave the candy in 30-second bursts until the candy is melted and slightly bubbling. (You can also bake them in an ovenproof container at 300°F/150°C for 8 to 10 minutes.) Avoid stirring the melted candy, as that will create bubbles. Be careful not to touch the melted candy with your skin, as it will be very hot.

Dip the Apple

Dip the apple into the melted candy, tilting it to cover the sides almost up to the top. Sprinkle it with edible glitter. Place on plate.

Decorate!

1. Roll a small piece of the white fondant to about ¼ inch (6 mm) thick to make teeth and eyes. Stick onto the apple.

2. Use food coloring of your choice to dye the rest of the fondant various colors to make the nose, mouth outline, eyes, eyebrows, and tuft of hair and stick them to the apple. Feel free to get creative here; none of us knows what aliens really look like. (Or—wait—do you?)

3. Use the colored fondant to create ears and antennae. Attach these to the apple using tooth-picks.

3, 2, 1 . . . Ya' done!

HIGH-FASHION DOLL CAKE

Season 3, Episode 6, "Ready to Wear, Ready to Eat"

Makes one 3-layer, 6-inch (15-cm) cake

Let your inner fashionista out with a stunning gown fit for the Met Gala you can eat! You can buy a half-doll body at craft stores, or just wrap your favorite full-size trendsetter's legs in plastic wrap and use her (or him!).

FOR THE CAKE

2½ cups (315 g) all-purpose flour

2 teaspoons baking powder

1 teaspoon baking soda

¼ teaspoon salt

4 large eggs

2 cups (400 g) sugar

⅔ cup (150 g) unsalted butter, melted

1 teaspoon vanilla extract

1 cup (240 ml) whole milk

FOR THE BUTTERCREAM

1 cup (2 sticks/225 g) unsalted butter, softened

4 cups (500 g) powdered sugar

2 teaspoons vanilla extract

⅛ teaspoon salt

¼ cup (60 ml) whole milk

FOR THE DECORATIONS

1 high-fashion doll

16 ounces (455 g) fondant color(s) of your choice

Cornstarch

Decorations of your choice, including fondant flowers, edible glitter, edible paint, and pressed pattern designs

SPECIAL EQUIPMENT

Three 6-inch (15-cm) round cake pans

Make the Cake

1. Preheat the oven to 350°F (175°C). Grease the cake pans. (If you're not quite on Jacques' level and you don't have three pans, fear not—you can bake in shifts, making sure to completely cool the pan between baking.) Cut out three 6-inch (15-cm) circles of parchment paper and place in the bottom of each pan.

2. In a large bowl, sift together the flour, baking powder, baking soda, and salt.

3. In another large bowl, using an electric mixer, combine the eggs, sugar, butter, vanilla, and milk. Add the dry mixture a spoonful at a time and mix until just combined. Do not overmix. Use a spatula to scrape the sides and bottom of the bowl to incorporate the last bits of dry ingredients.

4. Pour the batter into the pans, filling halfway (HALFWAY, PEOPLE), and bake for 24 to 28 minutes, until a toothpick inserted in the center comes out clean. Let cool.

Make the Buttercream

1. In a large bowl, using an electric mixer, beat the butter until creamy, about 1 minute.

2. Add the powdered sugar 1 cup (125 g) at a time, mixing until well combined.

3. Add the vanilla, salt, and milk, and mix on high until thick and creamy. If the buttercream is too thin, add more powdered sugar, 1 tablespoon at a time. If the buttercream is too thick, add more milk, 1 tablespoon at a time.

Assemble the Cake

1. Run a butter knife around the edge of the cake pans. Place a plate over the pan and flip. Tap the bottom until the cake slips out. Remove the parchment paper. Repeat for the remaining cakes. If a cake has a domed top, flip it over and cut it off with a large, serrated knife so the top is level.

2. Stack the cakes, spreading a layer of buttercream about ¼ to ½ inch (7 to 12 mm) thick between the layers to hold them in place. Using a large, serrated knife, sculpt the cake into a dome shape. Spread the remaining buttercream over the entire cake.

3. Stick the doll into the center of the cake.

Decorate!

1. Lightly dust a flat surface with cornstarch. Roll out the fondant to about ¼ inch (6 mm) thick and lay it over the top of the cake to make the dress. Smooth it down with your hands. Trim any excess from around the bottom. Use fondant to cover the torso of the doll.

2. Decorate the dress with fondant flowers, edible glitter, edible paint, pressed pattern designs, or anything your heart desires.

3, 2, 1 . . . Ya' done!

FROSTED TIP

Don't be stingy! Coat your pans thoroughly with cooking spray to prevent your cakes from sticking.

CLASSIC MARIA DOLL CAKE

¡Nailed It! México, Season 2, Episode 4, "Daft Craft"

Makes one 3-layer, 6-inch (15-cm) cake

In case you hadn't heard, *Nailed It!* has gone international, and this recipe comes to you from the kitchens of *¡Nailed It! México!* The classic Mexican Maria doll comes to life in this enchanting mini cake with a rice cereal head. Personalize yours with the skin, hair, eye, and dress color of your choice!

FOR THE CAKE

2½ cups (315 g) all-purpose flour

2 teaspoons baking powder

1 teaspoon baking soda

¼ teaspoon salt

4 large eggs

2 cups (400 g) sugar

⅔ cup (150 g) unsalted butter, melted

1 teaspoon vanilla extract

1 cup (240 ml) whole milk

FOR THE BUTTERCREAM

1 cup (2 sticks/225 g) unsalted butter, softened

4 cups (500 g) powdered sugar

2 teaspoons vanilla extract

⅛ teaspoon salt

¼ cup (60 ml) whole milk

FOR THE RICE CEREAL SHAPES

1 tablespoon butter

¾ cup (38 g) mini marshmallows

1 cup (15 g) crispy rice cereal

FOR THE DECORATIONS

Cornstarch

8 ounces (225 g) fondant, color of dress

4 ounces (115 g) fondant, dress accent color

4 ounces (115 g) fondant, ribbon #1 color

4 ounces (115 g) fondant, ribbon #2 color

4 ounces (115 g) fondant, color of skin

4 ounces (115 g) fondant, color of hair

12 inches (30.5 cm) edible lace

Edible paint in colors for lips and eyes

SPECIAL EQUIPMENT

Three 6-inch (15-cm) round cake pans

Food-safe paintbrush

Fondant tool or small sharp knife

1 lollipop stick or wooden dowel

Toothpicks

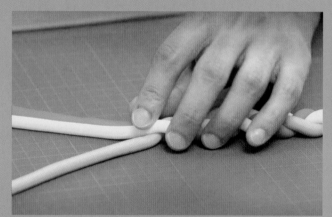

Make the Cake

1. Preheat the oven to 350°F (175°C). Grease the cake pans. (If you don't have 3 pans, you can bake in shifts, making sure to completely cool the pan between baking.) Cut out three 6-inch (15-cm) circles of parchment paper and place in the bottom of each pan.

2. In a large bowl, sift together the flour, baking powder, baking soda, and salt.

3. In another large bowl, using an electric mixer, combine the eggs, sugar, butter, vanilla, and milk. Add the dry mixture a spoonful at a time and mix until just combined. Do not overmix. Use a spatula to scrape the sides and bottom of the bowl to incorporate the last bits of dry ingredients.

4. Pour the batter into the pans, filling halfway, and bake for 24 to 28 minutes, until a toothpick inserted in the center comes out clean. Let cool.

Make the Buttercream

1. In a large bowl, using an electric mixer, beat the butter until creamy, about 1 minute.

2. Add the powdered sugar 1 cup (125 g) at a time, mixing until well combined.

3. Add the vanilla, salt, and milk, and mix on high until thick and creamy. If the buttercream is too thin, add more powdered sugar, 1 tablespoon at a time. If the buttercream is too thick, add more milk, 1 tablespoon at a time.

Make the Shaped Rice Cereal Head

1. In a small nonstick pot over medium-low, melt the butter.

2. Add the marshmallows and immediately take the pot off the heat. Stir continuously until the marshmallows melt. Stir in the rice cereal and mix until coated. (Enjoy the rush of childhood memories.) Pour the mixture onto a piece of parchment or foil on a flat surface and allow to cool.

3. When cool enough to handle, but not yet cold or too hard, scoop the mixture up and form it into a sphere about 3 inches (7.5 cm) in diameter. Press onto a flat surface to slightly flatten the back of the head. Set aside.

Assemble the Cake

1. Run a butter knife around the edge of the cake pans. Place a plate over the pan and flip. Tap the bottom until the cake slips out. Remove the parchment paper. Repeat for the remaining cakes. If a cake has a domed top, flip it over and cut it off with a large, serrated knife so the top is level. (You can snack on that excess for a delightful cake sample.)

2. Stack the cakes, spreading a layer of buttercream about ¼ to ½ inch (7 to 12 mm) thick between the layers to hold them in place. Using a large, serrated knife, sculpt the cake into a dome with a small circle on top for the torso. Spread the remaining buttercream over the entire cake.

FROSTED TIP

When putting multiple cake pans in the oven, make sure they are next to each other on the same rack, not above or below on different racks, or they won't cook evenly.

Dress the Doll in Fondant

1. Lightly dust a flat surface with cornstarch. Roll out the fondant for the main dress color. Wrap the torso in this color. Cut a large strip for the skirt; you can fold it back on itself to make pleats, if you'd like. Drape the skirt around the cake and trim the excess at the bottom.

2. Roll out the fondant for the dress accent colors and cut out thin stripes. Lightly wet the back of the strips with your finger dipped in water or using a paintbrush and attach them to the skirt. Use your fondant dress accent color to cut out 4 diamonds and attach them to the front of the dress. Wrap edible lace around the waist.

3. Use the dress color fondant to make arms. Attach them to the body of the cake using toothpicks stuck partially inside the arms and body so they're hidden from view. Add hands made from the skin color fondant.

Create the Doll's Face and Hair

1. Roll out the fondant for the skin color and wrap it around the rice cereal head. Add a small circle for the nose. Use a toothpick or sharp knife to press in a smile. Paint on lips and eyes. Add other fondant details, like eyelashes, eyebrows, and sparkles in the eyes.

2. Roll out the fondant for the hair color and add it to the head, scoring it with a fondant tool to resemble strands. Add pigtails.

3. Insert 1½ inches (4 cm) of the lollipop stick into the base of the head. Carefully stick the other side into the top of the doll's body.

4. Using three of your fondant colors, roll out ropes 12 inches (30.5 cm) long and braid them together. Attach the braid to the top of the doll's hair. Using those same colors, cut out strips ¼ by 1½ inches (6 by 40 mm) for the hair ribbons. Fold the strips into loops and attach them to the braid using water.

3, 2, 1 . . . Ya' done!

PANIC

FONDANT COLOR OVERWHELM

If you don't want to buy eight different fondant colors, you can always buy white and make your own shades using food coloring.

CAN'T FIND EDIBLE LACE

If you can't find edible lace at a cake supply store online, you can always make your own with fondant and a mold, or just improvise with a fondant ribbon.

ANTONI POROWSKI

The Montreal-born resident foodie from the television show *Queer Eye* stepped out of the kitchen to help judge his fellow castmates on a very special *Nailed It!* episode where they made cupcakes featuring their Fab selves.

▶ **How was your experience on the set?**

Nicole and Jacques could not have made us feel more comfortable or at home. Both complement each other so well and really bring out each other's funny side. It was a fun day and I hope to be back soon.

▶ **How would you describe yourself as a baker?**

I am notoriously impatient when it comes to baking. I leave it for special occasions like someone's birthday, a lazy Sunday, or when I have to apologize to someone. As much as I respect by-the-book bakers, I struggle with having the patience to measure and then wait while my dessert is in the oven.

▶ **What's your favorite dessert?**

Ina Garten's Beatty's Chocolate Cake is my favorite to make. My favorite to eat is a caramel *mazurek*: a traditional Polish Easter dessert that is a shortbread crust covered in a caramel layer, adorned with slivered almonds, and a bit of flaked salt.

▶ **What should a baker do if their dessert comes out looking terrible?**

Cover it with icing. Or powdered sugar. Laugh it off and carry on!

▶ **Any advice for home bakers?**

Be ready to make mistakes and embrace them. It's a natural part of the process, and you get to learn, hopefully, from each one you make.

ROCKET SHIP CAKE

Nailed It! At Home Experience

Makes one 2-layer rocket cake

This might be the most fun cake you ever make because you get to set it on fire! Be very careful when you do, though, since sugar is highly flammable. Created by Red Velvet NYC to commemorate the Netflix animated movie *Over the Moon*, this recipe was part of the second *Nailed It! At Home Experience* produced by Netflix and Fever.

FOR THE CAKE

1¼ cups (155 g) all-purpose flour

1 teaspoon baking powder

½ teaspoon baking soda

⅛ teaspoon salt

2 large eggs

1 cup (200 g) sugar

⅓ cup (75 g) unsalted butter, melted

½ teaspoon vanilla extract

½ cup (120 ml) whole milk

FOR THE BUTTERCREAM

1 cup (2 sticks/225 g) unsalted butter, room temperature, cut in chunks

4 cups (500 g) powdered sugar

2 teaspoons vanilla extract

⅛ teaspoon salt

2 tablespoons (30 ml) whole milk

FOR THE DECORATIONS

8 ounces (225 g) white fondant

Cornstarch

Red and blue food coloring

Rainbow sour belt candy

Rainbow Twizzlers or
Tootsie Roll Fruit Chews

SPECIAL EQUIPMENT

Small food-safe paintbrush

Rainbow candles

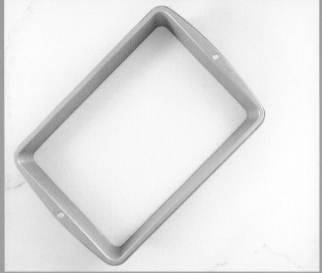

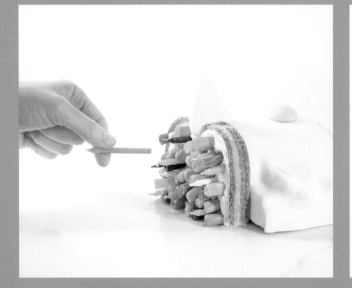

Make the Cake

1. Preheat the oven to 350°F (175°C). Grease a 9 by 13-inch (23 by 33-cm) baking pan. Cut out a rectangle of parchment paper the size of the pan and place it in the bottom.

2. In a medium bowl, sift together the flour, baking powder, baking soda, and salt.

3. In a large bowl, using an electric mixer, combine the eggs, sugar, butter, vanilla, and milk. Add the dry mixture a spoonful at a time and mix until just combined. Do not overmix. Use a spatula to scrape the sides and bottom of the bowl to incorporate the last bits of dry ingredients.

4. Pour the batter into the pan and bake for 16 to 18 minutes, until pale golden brown, or a toothpick inserted in the center comes out clean. Let cool.

Make the Buttercream

1. In a large bowl, using an electric mixer, beat the butter until creamy, about 1 minute.

2. Add the powdered sugar 1 cup (125 g) at a time, mixing until well combined.

3. Add the vanilla, salt, and milk, and mix on high until thick and creamy. If the buttercream is too thin, add more powdered sugar, 1 tablespoon at a time. If the buttercream is too thick, add more milk, 1 tablespoon at a time.

Assemble the Cake

1. Cut the sheet cake into 4 equal rectangles by slicing an X through the center of the cake. Stack 3 rectangles and set aside; they will form the body of the ship. Cut the last rectangle into 6 smaller pieces: 2 rectangles and 4 triangles. Stack one triangle on top of each small rectangle to form the wings. You'll have 2 spare triangles for snacking.

2. Using a spatula, spread a layer of buttercream about ¼ to ½ inch (7 to 12 mm) thick between the layers of the 3 large rectangles to hold them together. Using a large, serrated knife, trim the cake to form the spaceship, with a rounded body and a pointed nose. Place the wings at the sides. Spread the remaining buttercream over the entire ship, putting extra on the rear.

Decorate!

1. Break off a quarter of the fondant for the tail and windows and set aside. Lightly dust a flat surface with cornstarch and roll the remaining fondant into an oval about 12 inches (30.5 cm) wide. Lay the fondant over the top of the ship and smooth it down, leaving the rear of the ship uncovered. Trim any excess from the bottom.

2. Shape half of the reserved fondant into a triangle for the ship's tail. Slice a 1-inch (2.5-cm) opening to insert the tail.

3. Dye the rest of the fondant very pale blue. Roll it out and cut out windows. Use drops of water to "glue" the windows onto the ship.

4. Wrap the sour belts over the rear of the ship, trimming to fit. Use a small dab of buttercream to secure them. Cut Twizzlers into 2-inch (5-cm) pieces. Stuff the back of the ship with Twizzlers, Tootsie Rolls, and candles, making sure the candles are farther out so they don't light the other candy on fire.

5. Thin red food coloring in a little water and use it as paint to customize your rocket ship. Light the candles with adult supervision.

3, 2, 1 . . . Ya' done!

FROSTED TIP

If your fridge or freezer is big enough, place the stacked cake inside for 10 to 15 minutes before carving. A cool cake is much easier to carve!

CHOCOLATE ANIMAL MUD BATH

Season 1, Episode 3,
"Head Under Water"

Makes one 2-layer, 6-inch (15-cm) cake

Another Baker's Choice with different options for an adorable animal mud bath, this chocolate cake has chocolate buttercream and chocolate ganache on top. Customize using your favorite colors, flavors, and creature.

FOR THE CAKE

1 cup (125 g) all-purpose flour

¼ cup (25 g) unsweetened cocoa

1 teaspoon baking powder

½ teaspoon baking soda

⅛ teaspoon salt

2 large eggs

1 cup (200 g) sugar

⅓ cup (75 g) unsalted butter, melted

½ teaspoon vanilla extract

½ cup (120 ml) whole milk

FOR THE CHOCOLATE BUTTERCREAM

¾ cup (1½ sticks/170 g) unsalted butter, softened

⅓ cup (30 g) unsweetened cocoa

1 teaspoon vanilla extract

⅛ teaspoon salt

⅓ cup (55 g) semisweet chocolate chips, melted

4 cups (500 g) powdered sugar

¼ cup (60 ml) whole milk

FOR THE DECORATIONS

8 Kit Kat bars

8 ounces (225 g) fondant, color of your chosen animal

FOR THE GANACHE

8 ounces (225 g) dark chocolate, chopped

1 cup (240 ml) heavy cream

SPECIAL EQUIPMENT

Two 6-inch (15-cm) round cake pans

1 yard (91 cm) ribbon (If you prefer, you can make a ribbon out of extra white fondant colored to the ribbon color of your choice instead.)

Make the Cake

1. Preheat the oven to 325°F (165°C). Grease the cake pans. Cut out two 6-inch (15-cm) circles of parchment paper and place in the bottoms.

2. In a medium bowl, sift together the flour, cocoa, baking powder, baking soda, and salt.

3. In a large bowl, using an electric mixer, combine the eggs, sugar, butter, vanilla, and milk. Add the dry mixture a spoonful at a time and mix until just combined. Do not overmix. Use a spatula to scrape the sides and bottom of the bowl to incorporate the last bits of dry ingredients.

4. Pour the batter into the pans, filling halfway, and bake for 24 to 28 minutes, until a toothpick inserted in the center comes out clean. Let cool.

Make the Chocolate Buttercream

1. In a large bowl, using an electric mixer, beat the butter until creamy, about 1 minute.

2. Add the cocoa, vanilla, and salt and beat until smooth. Beat in the melted chocolate.

3. Add the powdered sugar 1 cup (125 g) at a time, mixing until well combined.

4. Add the milk and mix on high until thick and creamy. If the buttercream is too thin, add more powdered sugar, 1 tablespoon at a time. If the buttercream is too thick, add more milk, 1 tablespoon at a time.

Assemble the Cake

1. Run a butter knife around the edge of the cake pans. Place a plate over the pan and flip. Tap the bottom until the cake slips out. Remove the parchment paper. Repeat for the second cake. If a cake has a domed top, flip it over and cut it off with a large, serrated knife so the top is level.

2. With a spatula (an offset spatula works great if you have one), spread a layer of buttercream about ¼ to ½ inch (7 to 12 mm) thick on top of one cake. Place the other cake on top; press gently. Spread the remaining buttercream over the entire cake, making sure to give the sides enough to support the chocolate bars.

3. Break the Kit Kat bars apart and line them around the cake, standing upright, flat side toward the cake, as close together as possible.

Make the Fondant Animal

Use the fondant to shape animal parts—head, rump, feet.

Make the Ganache

1. Place the chocolate in a large heat-proof bowl. Set aside.

2. In a saucepan over medium, heat the cream until just bubbling. Remove from the heat and pour over the chocolate. Whisk until the chocolate melts and is fully combined. Allow to cool until it has a thick consistency.

3. Spoon the ganache over the top layer of the cake, keeping it inside the candy fence. (If there's any left over, grab a spoon and go to town on it. We won't tell.)

Decorate!

Arrange the animal parts inside the mud bath. Tie a ribbon around the candy bar fence to keep it all together, trimming ends as necessary. If you prefer, you can color some extra fondant and roll it to about ¼ inch (6 mm) thick to make a fondant ribbon instead. You can also use some extra fondant to create a towel for your soaking creature or any other accessories you can imagine!

3, 2, 1 . . . Ya' done!

LATE-NIGHT PANCAKE ART

Season 2, Episode 1, "High Society"

Makes 8 pancakes

We're leaving frosted cakes behind for a hot second for actual hot cakes shaped like frosted cakes. Or ice cream. Or cookies. All your favorite late-night munchies can get a morning makeover with this recipe thanks to colored batter and the griddle master's secret: squeeze bottles.

1¾ cups (220 g) all-purpose flour

1 tablespoon sugar

2 teaspoons baking powder

¼ teaspoon salt

2 large eggs

1¼ cups (300 ml) whole milk

4 tablespoons (½ stick/55 g) unsalted butter, melted

Red, orange, yellow, green, blue, brown food coloring (gel will give you brighter colors than liquid)

SPECIAL EQUIPMENT
Plastic squeeze bottles, one per batter color

1. In a large bowl, whisk together the flour, sugar, baking powder, and salt.

2. In a medium bowl, whisk together the eggs, milk, and butter. Carefully pour the wet mixture into the flour mixture and stir to remove all lumps. Try not to overmix.

3. Cut the tips of the plastic squeeze bottles to widen the openings for the thick pancake batter. Divide the batter among the squeeze bottles. Add a few drops of desired food coloring to each bottle and stir with a knife.

4. Heat a large griddle over medium-low heat. Very carefully to avoid touching the hot surface, wipe the griddle with olive oil on a paper towel to keep the pancakes from sticking.

5. To create a pancake picture, first "draw" the outlines with batter, then add details, then fill in the background with batter in the correct color. The design touching the pan first will be the main design after flipping; the side facing up now will be the bottom of the pancake, so what it looks like doesn't matter. Since the pancake will be flipped, be sure to write any words backward. For instance, to make a black-outlined heart pancake with the word "love" in it, first draw the outline of a heart with black batter, then squeeze out the letters "e v o l" backward.

6. Let the lines cook and firm up for a few seconds, then squeeze red batter inside the heart outline, over the top of the letters. Low heat and patience are the keys to pancake art. You'll know it's time to flip your creation when it's covered in bubbles and the surface of the batter is no longer shiny. When that happens, carefully flip it, allow it to cook for 30 seconds on the other side, then transfer it to a plate.

3, 2, 1 . . . Ya' done!

A retired transit officer from Abington, Massachusetts, this father of four and grandfather of two was so memorable during his first appearance—completely ignoring the instructions and almost setting the *Nailed It!* kitchen on fire—that we invited him back for more.

Baker Spotlight:
SAL VENTURELLI

Season 1, Episode 3, "Head Under Water" and Nailed It! Holiday! Season 1, Episode 6, "3 . . . 2 . . . 1, Ya Done!"

▶ **What's your favorite thing to bake?**

When I'm *allowed* to bake at home—believe me, it's *still* a disaster, even though I'm now a "world-renowned baker" (ha!)—my favorite is a layer cake. I mix it up with different types of cake, different frostings, and the filler is always a surprise.

▶ **What's your favorite dessert to eat?**

I *love* flan and crème brûlée. The quickest way into my heart is to make a nice custardy treat.

▶ **What was the best thing about being on *Nailed It!*?**

Being on the show was hugely exciting for me, but not for my wife, Dianne, who thinks that I'm the biggest ham ever. She *may* be right. Who knows? The trips out to LA to shoot the show were the best. The process of producing the show is *so* interesting. It takes something like four hours just to get one hour of final cut, and that's not including the one-on-one interview sections. I have a better respect now for the hard work that folks do in the entertainment industry.

▶ **Any behind-the-scenes secrets you can share?**

Okay, I'll give you one big secret . . . I made it home with the top hat from the holiday episode. I had to come home with *something*. If it wasn't $10,000, it was going to be THE HAT.

▶ **Are you ever recognized for being on the show?**

It's *unbelievable* how many people stop me to say hello, mostly kids, mostly in areas where a lot of people are gathered, like Boston's Logan Airport or a large train station. Some want to take pictures or "selfies" with me. It really makes people happy, so I'm glad to do it.

▶ **Any advice for home bakers?**

Push past failures because no one started out an expert. Try it again. I always think of Thomas Edison, who said: "I have not failed. I've just found ten thousand ways that won't work." Don't give up.

51

JUNGLE TOASTER PASTRIES

Season 4, Episode 5, "Jungle Bungle"

Makes 8 toaster pastries

The only thing better than Jacques' Tarzan yell is this jam-filled, jungle-themed treat. These homemade pastries are topped with a watery river made of royal icing, and one of them also has a crocodile made from modeling chocolate.

FOR THE PASTRIES

4 large egg yolks

¼ cup (60 ml) heavy cream

½ teaspoon vanilla extract

2 cups (250 g) all-purpose flour

1 tablespoon sugar

1 teaspoon salt

1 cup (2 sticks/225 g) unsalted butter, cold and cut into pieces

½ cup (120 ml) jam or preserves

FOR THE DECORATIONS

16 ounces (455 g) white modeling chocolate

Green and brown food coloring

FOR THE ROYAL ICING

1 cup (125 g) powdered sugar

2 teaspoons whole milk

2 teaspoons corn syrup

¼ teaspoon vanilla extract

Blue food coloring

Make the Pastries

1. In a small bowl, whisk together the yolks, heavy cream, and vanilla.

2. In a stand mixer with the paddle attachment, combine the flour, sugar, and salt. (We want it to look crumby now so it doesn't look crummy later.) Add the butter and mix until small crumbs form. Add the egg mixture and mix until a dough forms. Wrap the dough in plastic wrap and refrigerate for 20 minutes.

3. Preheat the oven to 350°F (175°C). (That's right, people, we're making toaster pastries in the oven! Life is full of contradictions. Just roll with it.) Line a baking sheet with parchment paper.

4. Lightly dust a flat surface with flour. Roll out the dough until it's ¼ inch (6 mm) thick. Cut sixteen 3 by 5-inch (7.5 by 12-cm) rectangles. Place half of the rectangles on the baking sheet. Spread 1 tablespoon jam into the center of each, keeping it away from the edges.

5. Using a brush or your finger dipped in water, wet the edges of one rectangle. Place another rectangle on top and seal the edges by pressing them together with the tines of a fork. Repeat for the remaining rectangles. Poke several holes in the top of each pastry to allow steam to escape. Bake for 10 to 15 minutes, until golden brown. Let cool on a wire rack.

Make the Crocodile

1. Knead the modeling chocolate until soft.

2. Pull off a marble-size piece and use it to form tiny (but terrifying) teeth. Set aside.

3. Pull off another marble-size piece and color it with brown food coloring. Roll out two spheres for eyes and cylinders for the tops of the reeds. Set aside.

4. Take the remainder of the modeling chocolate and form it into a flattened oval. Add a few drops of green food coloring to the middle, fold the sides of the chocolate over the color, then roll the chocolate between your palms to mix the color and form a long rope; as the rope grows, fold it in half and roll again. Continue until the color is evenly mixed. Make a few blades of grass using a couple of marble-size pieces and set aside. For the back of the crocodile, roll a golf ball–size sphere of chocolate, cut it in half, and score marks on the back of one side with a knife. Form the crocodile's head and open mouth just like you would with modeling clay, using the photo as a reference.

5. Using water as an adhesive, attach the eyes and teeth to the head, and attach the tops of the reeds to the grass.

Make the Royal Icing

1. Whisk the powdered sugar, milk, corn syrup, and vanilla together until smooth. If the icing is too thick, add a little water to thin it; if it's too thin, add a bit of powdered sugar. Add blue coloring. Stir as much or as little as you want to make a solid or more streaked color.

2. Spoon the icing into a piping bag. Draw the outline of the pond on a cooled pastry rectangle, then flood it with icing. Before the icing hardens, add the grass and crocodile to one of the pastries. If you like, for photo op purposes, you can arrange the pastries end-to-end so they form a long blue river with a crocodile lurking in the grassy area in the center.

3, 2, 1 . . . Ya' done!

GIANT EXOTIC PET CRACKER COOKIE

Season 6, Episode 1, "Im-Paw-Sible Cakes"

Makes 4 to 6 giant cookies

If you've ever wished those pink and white frosted animal crackers from your child-hood were *bigger*, we've got just the recipe for you! This extra-large sugar cookie is topped with royal icing and multicolored fondant balls.

FOR THE COOKIES

4½ cups (565 g) all-purpose flour

1 cup (220 g) brown sugar

1 cup (200 g) granulated sugar

1 tablespoon cornstarch

¾ teaspoon salt

¼ teaspoon baking powder

1 cup (1 stick/115 g) unsalted butter, softened

2 large eggs

2 teaspoons vanilla extract

1 tablespoon heavy cream

FOR THE ROYAL ICING

2 cups (250 g) powdered sugar

4 teaspoons whole milk

4 teaspoons corn syrup

1 teaspoon vanilla extract

Pink food coloring

FOR THE DECORATIONS

12 ounces (340 g) pink candy melts

12 ounces (340 g) white candy melts

4 ounces (115 g) white fondant

Red, yellow, green, and blue food coloring

SPECIAL EQUIPMENT

Large animal cookie cutter(s)

Make the Cookies

1. Preheat the oven to 350°F (175°C).

2. In a stand mixer with the paddle attachment, combine the flour, brown sugar, granulated sugar, cornstarch, salt, and baking powder. Add the butter and mix until a pebbly texture forms.

3. In a small bowl, whisk together the eggs, vanilla, and cream. Pour the wet mixture into the dry ingredients and mix until a soft dough forms. Remove half of the dough and set it aside. Add a few drops of pink food coloring to the remaining dough and mix until the dough is colored pink.

4. Lightly dust a flat surface with flour. Roll out each ball of dough to ½ inch (12 mm) thick. Use an oversize animal cookie cutter dipped in flour to cut out your animals. Place the animals on a nonstick or parchment-covered cookie sheet at least 2 inches (5 cm) apart.

5. Bake for 8 to 10 minutes, until the cookies are set but not browned. Remove from the oven and allow to cool on the pan for 5 minutes. Remove to a wire rack to completely cool. Resist the urge to chow down while they're warm (though if one disappears at this stage, that's your business).

Cover the Cookies in Candy Melts

1. Place the pink candy melts in a large microwave-safe bowl. Microwave in 10- to 15-second bursts, stirring after each, until the candy is almost, but not quite, melted. Stir to melt it completely. Spoon the melted candy onto the top of the cookies and smooth it with the back of the spoon. Let set on a cooling rack with a pan or parchment paper set underneath to catch drips.

2. Repeat with the white candy melts and the rest of the cookies.

Make the Royal Icing

1. Whisk the powdered sugar, milk, corn syrup, and vanilla together until smooth. You want it to be thick enough to stick to your finger. If the icing is too thin, add a bit of powdered sugar; if it's too thick, add a little water. Scoop half of the icing into a piping bag.

2. Add pink coloring to the remaining icing and mix. Spoon the pink icing into a piping bag. Cut a small hole into the end of both piping bags, about ⅛ inch (3 mm) wide.

Decorate!

1. Once the candy coating has hardened slightly, but not completely, use the white icing to outline the white cookies and add details. Do the same with the pink icing and pink cookies.

2. Divide the fondant into four pieces. Color one red, one yellow, one green, and one blue. Roll out small balls ⅛ inch (3 mm) thick. Lightly press the balls onto the surface of the cookies.

3, 2, 1 . . . Ya' done!

PANIC

CAN'T FIND GIANT COOKIE CUTTER

You can always find the outline of the animal of your choice online, print it out in a large size, cut it out, set it on top of the dough, and lightly trace the pattern with a toothpick. Then cut out your shape with a sharp knife dipped in flour.

GARDEN GNOME MINI PIE

Season 6. Episode 6.
"Everyone Romaine Calm"

Makes 1 to 2 mini pies

Our garden-themed episode wouldn't have been complete without an appearance from the *Gartenzwerg*, or garden gnome. Created in Germany to protect plant beds and give houses good luck, the wee creatures have found their way around the world—and onto these miniature pies.

FOR THE PIE DOUGH

2½ cups (315 g) all-purpose flour

2 tablespoons sugar

½ teaspoon salt

1 cup (205 g) butter-flavored shortening, cold, cut into cubes

6 tablespoons (90 ml) ice-cold water

FOR THE FILLING

One 4-ounce (115-g) box instant chocolate pudding mix

2 cups (480 ml) cold whole milk

SPECIAL EQUIPMENT

Mini pie pan (usually 5 inches/12.7 cm)

½ cup (200 g) dry beans or pie weights

Red, blue, white, brown, and skin color edible paint

Food-safe paintbrush

PANIC

PUDDING PRESSURE

Can't find pudding mix or don't want to make pudding? You can substitute a lunchbox-size pudding cup, custard, or any other filling of your choice.

Make the Pie Dough

1. Preheat the oven to 375°F (190°C). Grease the pie pan and place a narrow strip of parchment paper across the pan to assist with removing the baked crust later. (Our contestants probably could have benefited from this tip. Whoops.)

2. In a large bowl, whisk together the flour, sugar, and salt. Add the shortening cubes and, using a pastry cutter or two forks, cut the shortening into the mixture, scraping the sides of the bowl regularly, until the dough starts to get crumbly. Add water, one tablespoon at a time, mixing after each until the dough just comes together, then stop and discard any excess water you have left.

3. Lightly dust a flat surface with flour. Roll out the dough ⅛ inch (3 mm) thick. Cut a circle 2 inches (5 cm) wider than the pie pan, and gently lay the circular crust inside. Cut 3 strips ⅛ inch (3 mm) wide and 7 inches (17 cm) long. Braid them together and attach around the top edge of the pie crust.

4. Place a piece of parchment paper over the pie dough in the pan, and place the beans or pie weights on top (this will help hold the pie crust down while it's baking).

5. Bake 8 to 10 minutes, until the edges turn golden brown.

Make the Gnome, Mushroom & Lattice Top

1. Line a baking sheet with parchment paper.

2. Gather the leftover pie dough and roll it out ⅛ inch (3 mm) thick.

3. Cut out a 2-inch (5-cm) wide, 3-inch (7.5-cm) tall garden gnome and 1-inch (2.5-cm) wide and tall mushroom shape, leaving a tab of dough on the bottom of each to insert into the pie. Place on the baking sheet.

4. Cut eight strips of dough about ¾ inch (2 cm) wide and weave them together to make a lattice top 6 inches (15 cm) across, and cut it into a half circle. Place on the baking sheet.

5. Bake 8 to 10 minutes, until the shapes turn golden brown.

6. Once they're completely cool, use the edible paints to give the gnome and mushroom detail and color. Let dry.

Make the Filling

In a medium bowl, whisk together the pudding mix and milk until combined, about 2 minutes. Refrigerate for 5 to 10 minutes, until the pudding is softly set.

Assemble the Pie

Remove the pie crust from the pie pan and place on a plate. Spoon filling into the crust. Lay the lattice top over one half of the pie, then stick the gnome into the filling and the mushroom into the lattice top. If you're feeling creative, you can add grass, flowers, or any other decorations you want to complete your garden scene, using the steps to make royal icing from the previous recipe (page 55) colored however you like.

3, 2, 1 . . . Ya' done!

SERIOUS CHALLENGES WHERE MASTERPIECES CAN EASILY BECOME DISASTERPIECES.

BUT FEAR NOT, FOR WHILE THE RECIPES MIGHT BE LARGE, THEY HOLD GIANT AMOUNTS OF FUN! AND WILL UNDOUBTEDLY RESULT IN A . . . CREATION. OF SOME SORT. WORTHY OF PUBLIC ADMIRATION AND PRAISE. WHICH WE WILL HAPPILY SHARE IF YOU POST YOUR CREATION TO SOCIAL MEDIA WITH

GOOD LUCK!

NAIL IT
OR
FAIL IT

VOLCANO CAKE

Season 1, Episode 4, "Weird Science"

Makes one 3-tier, 5-layer volcano cake

The science project of your childhood dreams becomes a dangerously delicious dessert in this mountain of chocolate cake that sizzles and smokes. To keep this prehistoric diorama standing, we'll add cake boards and wooden dowels for support.

FOR THE CAKE

4 cups (500 g) all-purpose flour

1 cup (95 g) unsweetened cocoa

4 teaspoons baking powder

2 teaspoons baking soda

½ teaspoon salt

8 large eggs

4 cups (800 g) sugar

2 cups (480 ml) whole milk

1 cup (240 ml) vegetable oil

FOR THE BUTTERCREAM

2 cups (4 sticks/450 g) unsalted butter, softened

8 cups (1 kg) powdered sugar

4 teaspoons vanilla extract

¼ teaspoon salt

¼ cup (60 ml) whole milk

Red, green, and blue food coloring

FOR THE DECORATIONS

16 ounces (455 g) white modeling chocolate

Green and brown food coloring

Four graham crackers

SPECIAL EQUIPMENT

Two 10-inch (25-cm) round cake pans

Two 8-inch (20-cm) round cake pans

One 6-inch (15-cm) round cake pan

Cake base or three 12-inch (30.5-cm) cake boards taped together and wrapped in foil

One 8-inch (20-cm) round cake board

One 6-inch (15-cm) round cake board

Nine cake dowel rods

Burlap ribbon or fabric strip, about 39 inches (1 meter) long

Glass candle votive

Toothpicks

Dry ice

> **PANIC**
>
> ## FROSTING OVERLOAD
>
> **Exploding volcanoes require a lot of buttercream. If you're not keen to make 10 cups (2.4 L) of it yourself, you can save time by buying it premade. You'll need 3 cans of green frosting, 1 can of blue, and 1 can of red, based on a typical can size of around 16 ounces (453 g).**

Make the Cake

1. Since most kitchen mixers can't accommodate the batter for five cakes at once, we're going to split the job in half.

2. Preheat the oven to 325°F (165°C). Grease the cake pans. Cut out a circle of parchment paper for each pan and place in the bottom of each.

3. In a large bowl, sift together 2 cups (250 g) of the flour, ½ cup (50 g) of the cocoa, 2 teaspoons of the baking powder, 1 teaspoon of the baking soda, and ⅛ teaspoon of the salt.

4. In another large bowl, using an electric mixer or whisk, combine 4 of the eggs, 2 cups (400 g) of the sugar, 1 cup (240 ml) of the milk, and ½ cup (120 ml) of the vegetable oil. Add the dry mixture a large spoonful at a time and mix until just combined. Do not overmix. Use a spatula to scrape the sides and bottom of the bowl to incorporate the last bits of dry ingredients. Divide the batter between the two 10-inch (25-cm) pans, filling halfway.

5. Repeat with the remaining cake ingredients, dividing the batter among the remaining three cake pans.

6. Bake for 24 to 28 minutes, until a toothpick inserted in the center comes out clean. Let cool. (Seriously, PLEASE let your cakes cool before you try to decorate them, and thank us later.)

Make the Buttercream

1. We need a *lot* of buttercream for this recipe, and most mixers can't handle this much powdered sugar at one time, so we'll make it in two batches.

2. In a large bowl, using an electric mixer, beat 1 cup (2 sticks/225 g) of the butter until creamy, about 1 minute.

3. Add 4 cups (500 g) of the powdered sugar 1 cup (125 g) at a time, mixing until well combined.

4. Add 2 teaspoons of the vanilla, ⅛ teaspoon of the salt, and 2 tablespoons (30 ml) of the milk, and mix on high until thick and creamy. If the buttercream is too thin, add more powdered sugar, 1 tablespoon at a time. If the buttercream is too thick, add more milk, 1 tablespoon at a time.

5. Repeat with the remaining buttercream ingredients to make a second batch.

6. Scoop out 2 cups (480 ml) of white buttercream and set aside.

7. Fill two small bowls or ramekins each with 1 cup (240 ml) of buttercream. Color one bowl with red food coloring for the lava. Color the other bowl with blue food coloring for the water. Color the remaining buttercream in the original bowl green. Set aside half of the green buttercream to make vegetation. Set the other colored buttercreams aside.

FROSTED TIP

For less disgusting results, never frost your cakes with your hands. (You'd think we wouldn't need to say that, but we've seen a lot on this show.)

If you can fit your cake in the freezer and let it chill for 30 minutes after you've stacked it, it will be much easier to carve.

Assemble the Cake

1. Place a dab of white buttercream on the center of the cake base.

2. Run a butter knife around the edge of one of the 10-inch (25-cm) cake pans. Place a plate over the pan and flip. Tap the bottom until the cake slips out. Remove the parchment paper. If the cake has a domed top, flip it over and cut it off with a large, serrated knife so the top is level. Set the cake on the center of the cake base. Spread a thin layer of white buttercream on top, leaving a 1-inch (2.5-cm) border bare. Repeat for the second 10-inch (25-cm) cake, placing it on top of first cake and frosting it, but leaving 2 inches (5 cm) around the outside bare.

3. Lightly set the 8-inch (20-cm) cake board on the center of the cake stack and trace its outline into the cake surface with a knife or toothpick so you know where it will go, then set aside. Hold a dowel next to the cake and mark the height on the dowel. Cut five dowels to that length. Press one dowel into the center of the cake and press four more around it, spacing them out for support, but staying at least ½ inch (12 mm) within the traced circle. Place the 8-inch (20-cm) cake board back on top of the stack inside the traced circle and lightly press down. Place a dab of buttercream on the center of the cake board.

4. Remove the 8-inch (20-cm) cakes from their pans and stack them, one at a time, on top of the 10-inch (25-cm) cakes, cutting their tops to be level if necessary, and spreading a thin layer of buttercream on top of each layer.

5. Lightly set the 6-inch (15-cm) cake board on top of the cake stack and trace its outline with a knife or toothpick. Remove the cake board. Hold a dowel next to the cake with the bottom aligned with the 8-inch cake board and mark the remaining height on the dowel. Cut four dowels to that length. Press the dowels into the cake, spacing them out for support, but staying at least ½ inch (12 mm) inside the traced circle. Place the cake board back in the circle and lightly press down. Place a dab of buttercream on the center of the cake board.

6. Remove the 6-inch (15-cm) cake from its pan and place it on top. Carve a small hole in the very top and insert the glass votive.

7. Using a large, serrated knife, sculpt the cake into a dome, starting at the top and sloping downward, using the two cake board sizes as a guide to the slope. Cover the entire cake in green buttercream, but don't frost over the top of the glass votive.

PANIC

DAUNTED BY DINOS

While the modeling chocolate creatures are super fun, plastic toy dinosaurs and palm trees found at party and craft stores are the perfect size for this cake and can be easily substituted. And you'll have a permanent reminder of your historic creation to play with afterward!

DRY ICE ALTERNATIVE

If you don't want to use dry ice for the Volcano Cake, you can skip the glass votive in the top of the cake and replace it with sparkling candles.

Make the Trees and Dinosaurs

1. Break off a tennis ball–size piece of the modeling chocolate. Knead it until soft, then form it into a flattened oval. Add a few drops of brown food coloring to the middle, fold the sides of the chocolate over the color, then roll the chocolate between your palms to mix the color and form a long rope; as the rope grows, fold it in half and roll again. Continue until the color is evenly mixed. Roll out tree trunks and boulders with some of the brown, and make dinosaurs with the rest.

2. Break off a tennis ball–size piece of the modeling chocolate, knead it until soft, then color it green using the method above. Roll out some to about ¼ inch (6 mm) thick, and cut it into palm tree leaves; form the rest into a dinosaur.

3. Using water as an adhesive, attach eyes and details formed from tiny bits of modeling chocolate to the dinosaurs, and the leaves to the tree trunks.

Decorate!

1. Fill a piping bag with the blue buttercream and pipe a waterfall down one side of the cake.

2. Fill another piping bag with red buttercream, and draw lava dripping from the top of the cake, being sure to leave the votive open.

3. Place the boulders, trees, and dinosaurs on the cake, securing them with toothpicks.

4. Fill a piping bag with the remaining green buttercream, and add grassy details around the trees, dinosaurs, and waterfall.

5. Crush graham crackers into crumbs and add them to the banks of the river as sand.

6. Wrap the bottom of the cake base with burlap.

Ignite the Volcano

With adult supervision and extreme caution, place a few pieces of dry ice into the glass votive. Slowly pour a small amount of warm water into the glass to create a smoking effect. Be careful not to add too much water—you don't want the votive to overflow and turn your cake into a soggy wet mess. (Though we're no strangers to soggy wet messes!)

DRY ICE SAFETY TIPS

- Never touch dry ice with your bare hands or allow it to touch any exposed skin.

- Use protective gloves and tongs to handle dry ice.

- Do not inhale the fumes of dry ice or use it in a poorly ventilated area.

- Do not leave children unattended around dry ice.

- Do not attempt to eat dry ice.

- To dispose of dry ice, pour warm water over it in a well-ventilated area until it fully melts.

- Do not throw unmelted dry ice in the trash or down your sink.

UNICORN CAKE

Season 2, Episode 2, "Fictitious and Delicious"

Makes one 5-layer, 6-inch (15-cm) unicorn cake

The dessert that launched a thousand fails: the mythical, magical, rainbow unicorn cake! This one has a luxurious chocolate ganache mane decorated with pastel flowers and a glorious golden fondant horn.

FOR THE CAKE

5 cups (625 g) all-purpose flour

4 teaspoons baking powder

2 teaspoons baking soda

½ teaspoon salt

8 large eggs

4 cups (800 g) sugar

2 cups (480 ml) whole milk

1½ cups (360 ml) vegetable oil

2 teaspoons vanilla extract

Red, orange, yellow, green, blue, and purple food coloring

FOR THE BUTTERCREAM

2 cups (4 sticks/450 g) unsalted butter, room temperature, cut into chunks

8 cups (1 kg) powdered sugar

4 teaspoons vanilla extract

¼ teaspoon salt

¼ cup (60 ml) whole milk

Red, yellow, green, and blue food coloring

FOR THE GANACHE

4 ounces (112 g) dark chocolate, chopped

½ cup + 2 tablespoons (150 ml) heavy cream

FOR THE DECORATIONS

8 ounces (225 g) gold fondant

4 ounces (115 g) white fondant

4 ounces (115 g) black fondant

SPECIAL EQUIPMENT

Five 6-inch (15-cm) round cake pans

One 10-inch (25-cm) round cake board

1 bamboo or wooden skewer

 CAN'T FIND GOLD FONDANT

PANIC

If you can't find gold fondant, you can use yellow. Or pink. You could also use white fondant and cover it with edible glitter or spray it with food-safe gold color.

Make the Cake

1. Since most kitchen mixers can't accommodate the batter for five cakes at once, we're going to split the job in half.

2. Preheat the oven to 350°F (175°C). Grease the cake pans. Cut out five 6-inch (15-cm) circles of parchment paper and place in the bottom of each pan. (If you don't have five pans, you can bake in shifts, making sure to completely cool the pan between baking.)

3. In a large bowl, sift together 2½ cups (315 g) of the flour, 2 teaspoons of the baking powder, 1 teaspoon of the baking soda, and ¼ teaspoon of the salt.

4. In another large bowl, using an electric mixer or whisk, combine 4 of the eggs, 2 cups (400 g) of the sugar, 1 cup (240 ml) of the milk, ¾ cup (180 ml) of the vegetable oil, and 1 teaspoon of the vanilla. Add the dry mixture a large spoonful at a time and mix until just combined. Do not overmix. Use a spatula to scrape the sides and bottom of the bowl to incorporate the last bits of dry ingredients. Set aside. Repeat with the remaining cake ingredients to make the second batch.

5. Divide the batter equally between 5 bowls. Color one bowl of batter red, one yellow, one green, one blue, and one purple. Fill each cake pan halfway with a single colored batter.

6. Bake for 24 to 28 minutes, until a toothpick inserted in the center comes out clean. Let cool.

Make the Buttercream

1. We need a *lot* of buttercream for this recipe, and most mixers can't handle this much powdered sugar at one time, so we'll make it in two batches.

2. In a large bowl, using an electric mixer, beat 1 cup (2 sticks/225 g) of the butter until creamy, about 1 minute.

3. Add 4 cups (500 g) of the powdered sugar 1 cup (125 g) at a time, mixing until well combined.

4. Add 2 teaspoons of the vanilla, ⅛ teaspoon of the salt, and 2 tablespoons (30 ml) of the milk, and mix on high until thick and creamy. If the buttercream is too thin, add more powdered sugar, 1 tablespoon at a time. If the buttercream is too thick, add more milk, 1 tablespoon at a time.

5. Repeat with the remaining buttercream ingredients to make a second batch.

6. Fill four small bowls or ramekins each with ¾ cup (180 ml) of buttercream. Color one bowl with yellow food coloring, one bowl with green food coloring, one bowl with red food coloring to make pink, and one bowl with blue food coloring. Cover each bowl with plastic wrap and set aside.

PANIC

CAN'T FACE IT

If you don't fancy making the eyes and horn, many cake and craft stores now sell these very accessories that can be stuck directly into your beautiful beast.

Assemble the Cake

1. Place a dab of white buttercream on the center of the cake base.

2. Run a butter knife around the edge of the pan with the purple cake. Place a plate over the pan and flip. Tap the bottom until the cake slips out. Remove the parchment paper. If the cake has a domed top, flip it over and cut it off with a large, serrated knife so the top is level. Set the cake on the center of the cake base. With a spatula (an offset spatula works great if you have one), spread a layer of white buttercream about ¼ to ½ inch (7 to 12 mm) thick on top. Repeat with the blue cake, then green, yellow, orange, and red.

3. Carefully place the stacked cake in the fridge for 20 minutes to chill, then take it out and cover the entire cake in white buttercream, making the edges as smooth as possible. (Ideally, they'll be about as smooth as Nicole flirting.)

Make the Ganache

1. Place the dark chocolate in a large heat-proof bowl.

2. In a saucepan over medium, heat the cream until just bubbling. Remove from the heat and pour over the chocolate. Whisk until fully combined. Allow to cool until it has a thick consistency but is still slightly warm.

3. Using a large spoon, drizzle the ganache in a circle around the top of the cake, allowing it to drip down the sides. Fill in the circle to cover the top of the cake and smooth it with an offset spatula.

Make the Unicorn Horn and Eyes

1. Roll the gold fondant into a rope that is thicker on one end than the other. Place the bamboo skewer at the tip of the thinner end, and wrap the fondant around the skewer, creating the unicorn horn. Continue two-thirds of the way down the skewer, and then stop. Stick the horn into the cake.

2. Lightly dust a flat surface with cornstarch. Roll out the white fondant to about ¼ inch (6 mm) thick and cut out ovals for the unicorn's eyes. Roll up the fondant scraps and dye them blue for the unicorn's irises. Roll the blue fondant out and cut it into shape. Use drops of water to "glue" the irises to the eyes. Press the assembled eyes into the frosting on the cake.

3. Roll out the black fondant to about ¼ inch (6 mm) thick and cut it into thin eyeliner and eyelashes for the unicorn's eyes. Use drops of water to "glue" them in place.

Decorate!

Fit a piping bag with a decorative tip. Hold the piping bag open and carefully spoon in one scoop of each of the colored buttercreams around and inside the edge. Push the buttercream down, then twist the bag closed. The buttercream will come out multicolored. Add flowers and swirls to the unicorn cake for the mane and other details.

3, 2, 1 . . . Ya' done!

> ## FROSTED TIP
> Cool your cakes before frosting or drizzling with ganache, or you'll melt the buttercream. The scientific term for cake covered in melted buttercream is "a hot mess."

SWEET EXPLOSION CAKE

¡Nailed It! México, Season 1, Episode 5, "Sweet Explosion"

Makes one 4-layer, 6-inch (15-cm) cake

Inspired by sprinkles aficionado and guest judge Amirah Kassem, this tie-dye cake is a sweet explosion of color and candy. While it looks real, all of the candy on and around the cake is actually made of fondant.

FOR THE CAKE

2½ cups (315 g) all-purpose flour

2 teaspoons baking powder

1 teaspoon baking soda

¼ teaspoon salt

4 large eggs

2 cups (400 g) sugar

⅔ cup (150 g) unsalted butter, melted

1 teaspoon vanilla extract

1 cup (240 ml) whole milk

Yellow, green, blue, purple, and pink food coloring

FOR THE BUTTERCREAM

1 cup (2 sticks/225 g) unsalted butter, room temperature, cut into chunks

4 cups (500 g) powdered sugar

2 teaspoons vanilla extract

⅛ teaspoon salt

2 tablespoons (30 ml) whole milk

FOR THE DECORATIONS

One 1½-ounce (45-ml) can color mist food spray in orange, yellow, green, blue, and purple

12 ounces (340 g) orange-colored candy melts

16 ounces (455 g) white fondant

4 ounces (115 g) black fondant

SPECIAL EQUIPMENT

Four 6-inch (15-cm) round cake pans

One 10-inch (25-cm) round cake board

Colored paper drink straws (for the fondant lollipops)

PANIC

NOT CRAZY ABOUT FONDANT CANDY

Super easy: Substitute real candy and macarons instead.

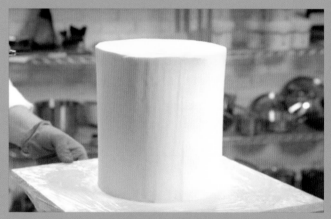

Make the Cake

1. Preheat the oven to 350°F (175°C). Grease the cake pans. (If you don't have four pans, you can bake in shifts, making sure to completely cool the pan between baking.)

2. In a medium bowl, sift together the flour, baking powder, baking soda, and salt.

3. In a large bowl, using an electric mixer or whisk, combine the eggs, sugar, butter, vanilla, and milk. Add the dry mixture a large spoonful at a time and mix until just combined. Do not overmix. Use a spatula to scrape the sides and bottom of the bowl to incorporate the last bits of dry ingredients.

4. Divide the batter evenly among 5 different containers. Color one yellow, one green, one blue, one purple, and one pink with food coloring. Pour a bit of each color batter into each cake pan, so that each pan has five different sections of colored batter, filling each halfway. Using a spatula, gently swirl the batter just once to slightly mix the colors. Do not overmix, or the resulting color will be a muddy mess rather than a fun tie-dye.

5. Bake for 16 to 18 minutes, until a toothpick inserted in the center comes out clean. Let cool.

COLOR MIST TIPS

- Shake the can well before using.

- Use in a well-ventilated area.

- Cover your work area in paper because the spray tends to splatter.

- Practice first by spraying on a piece of paper to get used to it.

- Don't spray too closely or too much. The best distance is 6 to 8 inches (15 to 20 cm) from your surface using light, sweeping strokes.

- After spraying, let the surface dry for 10 minutes before touching it.

Make the Buttercream

1. In a large bowl, using an electric mixer, beat the butter until creamy, about 1 minute.

2. Add the powdered sugar 1 cup (125 g) at a time, mixing until well combined.

3. Add the vanilla, salt, and milk, and mix on high until thick and creamy. If the buttercream is too thin, add more powdered sugar, 1 tablespoon at a time. If the buttercream is too thick, add more milk, 1 tablespoon at a time.

Assemble the Cake

1. Place a dab of buttercream on the center of the cake board.

2. Run a butter knife around the edge of one of the cake pans. Place a plate over the pan and flip. Tap the bottom until the cake slips out. If the cake has a domed top, flip it over and cut it off with a large, serrated knife so the top is level. Set the cake on the center of the cake base. With a spatula (an offset spatula works great if you have one), spread a layer of buttercream about ¼ to ½ inch (7 to 12 mm) thick on top. Repeat with the remaining cakes.

3. Cover the entire cake in buttercream, making the edges as smooth as possible.

4. Spray a band around the side, near the top of the cake, with yellow color mist. Spray a band of orange next. Continue spraying color stripes down the side: purple, then blue, then green on the bottom.

Make the Candy Drizzle

1. Place the candy melts in a large microwave-safe bowl. Microwave in 10- to 15-second bursts, stirring after each, until the candy is almost, but not quite, melted. Stir to melt it completely.

2. Pour the melted topping around the top edge of the cake, allowing it to drip down the sides. Cover the top of the cake with the rest of the drizzle.

Make the Face

1. Pinch off a marble-size piece of white fondant, knead it to soften, then color it red. Do the same to make blue fondant.

2. Lightly dust a flat surface with cornstarch. Roll the black fondant out and cut out two circles about 1 inch (2.5 cm) tall for the eyes. Roll out the white fondant and cut two circles just slightly smaller than the black circles. Roll out the blue fondant and cut two smaller circles. Cut two black circles just slightly smaller than the blue circles. Cut two tiny white circles. Use water to "glue" the eye pieces in a stack, using the photo as a reference. Add black eyelashes and eyebrows and stick them all to the cake.

3. Cut out a piece of white fondant in the shape of the mouth and a slightly smaller piece of black fondant in the same shape. Use water to "glue" the black piece on top of the white to form a black mouth with a white outline and attach it to the cake. Form a tiny red tongue and attach it to the mouth.

Make the Candy

Dye the remaining white fondant whatever colors you choose to make the candy decorations. Roll the colors into long strips, then twist the strips together, and coil them to make lollipops. Make macarons by cutting out two small circles of one color and sandwiching them around a circle of another color. Add fondant gumballs and gumdrops. Use colored paper drinking straws as lollipop sticks. Add your fondant candy to top of the cake.

3, 2, 1 . . . Ya' done!

RON FUNCHES

Comedian Ron Funches, best known to many young viewers as the voice of Cooper in the *Trolls* franchise, was a special guest judge on the holiday episode "Toying Around," where he showcased his talent for robot dancing, and returned for Double Trouble episode 2, "The Burbank State Fair."

▶ **Can you bake?**

I can bake a cake out of a box and a mean mac 'n' cheese. Those are my limits.

▶ **Who taught you?**

I learned my mac 'n' cheese from my mom and then perfected it on my own.

▶ **What's your favorite dessert to eat?**

I love a mixed berry cobbler.

▶ **Any advice for home bakers?**

Have fun and enjoy. The best part about baking is that you can still eat your mistakes. I wish the rest of life worked that way.

SYLVIA WEINSTOCK WEDDING CAKE

Season 1, Episode 1, "First Date to Life Mate"

Makes one 3-tier, 7-layer cake

If you watched the very first episode of *Nailed It!* and thought "I can do that," now's your chance to prove it. This dreamy wedding cake looks straightforward enough, but it does have quite a few steps and different techniques: from painting on buttercream and sculpting modeling chocolate to making sugar flowers. The key to large, structured cakes like this one is good support and stabilization provided by hidden cake boards and dowels.

FOR THE CAKE

7½ cups (875 g) all-purpose flour

2 tablespoons baking powder

1 tablespoon baking soda

1 teaspoon salt

12 large eggs

6 cups (1.2 kg) sugar

3 cups (720 ml) whole milk

2¼ cups (540 ml) vegetable oil

1 tablespoon vanilla extract

FOR THE BUTTERCREAM

2 cups (4 sticks/450 g) unsalted butter, room temperature, cut into chunks

8 cups (1 kg) powdered sugar

4 teaspoons vanilla extract

¼ teaspoon salt

¼ cup (60 ml) whole milk

Teal food coloring

FOR THE DECORATIONS

Brown edible cake paint

8 ounces (225 g) brown modeling chocolate

4 ounces (115 g) black modeling chocolate

16 ounces (455 g) white gum paste

Green food coloring

Cornstarch

SPECIAL EQUIPMENT

Two 10-inch (25-cm) round cake pans

Three 8-inch (20-cm) round cake pans

Two 6-inch (15-cm) round cake pans

Cake base or three 14-inch (35.5-cm) cake boards taped together and wrapped in foil

One 8-inch (20-cm) round cake board

One 6-inch (15-cm) round cake board

Nine cake dowel rods

Cake decorating stencils

Food-safe paintbrush

Toothpicks

Food-safe floral wire

Small block of Styrofoam

Make the Cake

1. Since most kitchen mixers can't accommodate the batter for seven cakes at once, we're going to split the job in half.

2. Preheat the oven to 350°F (175°C). Grease the cake pans. Cut out a circle of parchment paper for each pan and place in the bottom of each pan. (If you don't have enough of a certain size pan, you can bake in shifts, making sure to completely cool the pan between baking.)

3. In a large bowl, sift together 3¾ cups (438 g) of the flour, 1 tablespoon of the baking powder, 1½ teaspoons of the baking soda, and ½ teaspoon of the salt.

4. In another large bowl, using an electric mixer, combine 6 of the eggs, 3 cups (600 g) of the sugar, 1½ cups (360 ml) of the milk, 1 cup plus 2 tablespoons (270 ml) of the vegetable oil, and 1½ teaspoons of the vanilla. Add the dry mixture a large spoonful at a time and mix until just combined. Do not overmix. Use a spatula to scrape the sides and bottom of the bowl to incorporate the last bits of dry ingredients.

5. Pour the batter into one 10-inch (25-cm) pan and two 8-inch (20-cm) pans, filling halfway.

6. Repeat with the remaining cake ingredients, filling the three remaining pans halfway.

7. Bake for 20 to 28 minutes, until a toothpick inserted in the center comes out clean. Let cool.

Make the Buttercream

1. We need a *lot* of buttercream for this recipe, and most mixers can't handle this much powdered sugar at one time, so we'll make it in two batches.

2. In a large bowl, using an electric mixer, beat 1 cup (2 sticks/225 g) of the butter until creamy, about 1 minute.

3. Add 4 cups (500 g) of the powdered sugar 1 cup (125 g) at a time, mixing until well combined.

4. Add 2 teaspoons of the vanilla, ⅛ teaspoon of the salt, and 2 tablespoons (30 ml) of the milk, and mix on high until thick and creamy. If the buttercream is too thin, add more powdered sugar, 1 tablespoon at a time. If the buttercream is too thick, add more milk, 1 tablespoon at a time.

5. Repeat with the remaining buttercream ingredients to make a second batch.

6. Use a few drops of teal food coloring to tint the buttercream a very light, pale blue.

PANIC

THOSE AREN'T REAL FLOWERS?

Nope, they're made entirely of gum paste, which is an entire project on its own that people like Sylvia have dedicated years to perfecting. Anything you make is going to be lovely, but if you prefer to skip this step, you can always purchase some live flowers, wrap their stems in foil, poke them right into the cake top, and finish strong with a little help from Mother Nature!

Assemble the Cake

1. Place a dab of buttercream on the center of the cake base.

2. Run a butter knife around the edge of one of the 10-inch (25-cm) cake pans. Place a plate over the pan and flip. Tap the bottom until the cake slips out. Remove the parchment paper. If the cake has a domed top, flip it over and cut it off with a large, serrated knife so the top is level. (Domed cakes lead to wobbly cakes, which lead to tipped over cakes, which lead to heartbreak. And that won't do—this is supposed to be a wedding cake, after all.) Set the cake on the center of the cake base. With a spatula (an offset spatula works great if you have one), spread a layer of buttercream about ¼ to ½ inch (7 to 12 mm) thick on top. Repeat with the remaining 10-inch (25-cm) cake.

3. Lightly set the 8-inch (20-cm) cake board on the center of the cake stack and trace its outline with a knife or toothpick so you know where it will go. Remove the cake board. Hold a dowel next to the cake and mark the height on the dowel. Cut five dowels to that length. Press one dowel into the center of the cake and press four more down around it, spacing them out for support, but staying at least ½ inch (12 mm) within the traced circle. Place the 8-inch (20-cm) cake board back in the circle and lightly press down. Place a dab of buttercream on the center of the cake board.

4. Remove the 8-inch (20-cm) cakes from their pans and stack them, one at a time, on top of the stack, cutting their tops to be level if necessary, and spreading a layer of buttercream about ¼ to ½ inch (7 to 12 mm) thick on top of each layer.

5. Lightly set the 6-inch (15-cm) cake board on top of the cake stack and trace its outline with a knife or toothpick. Remove the cake board. Hold a dowel next to the cake and mark the height on the dowel. Cut four dowels to that length. Press the dowels into the cake, spacing them out for support, but staying at least ½ inch (12 mm) inside the traced circle. Place the cake board back in the circle and lightly press down. Place a dab of buttercream on the center of the cake board.

6. Remove the 6-inch (15-cm) cakes from their pans and add them, one at a time, on top of the stack, cutting their tops to be level if necessary, and spreading a layer of buttercream on top of each layer.

7. Cover the entire cake in buttercream, making the edges as smooth as possible. Let the cake sit for at least 30 minutes until the buttercream is firm.

Stencil the Cake

Stick the stencil onto the cake where you want it by placing it very lightly against the buttercream. Use a brush and paint the stencil in with the edible paint; don't use too much or it might bleed under the stencil. Remove the stencil.

Make the Bows

Knead the brown modeling chocolate until soft. Roll out a section ¼ inch (6 mm) thick and cut out a 2 by 6-inch (5 by 15-cm) rectangle and a 1½ by ½-inch (40 by 12-mm) rectangle. Take the larger rectangle and fold the short ends back to make a loop. Gently squeeze the loop in the middle to form a bow. Wrap the smaller rectangle around the center to secure the bow. Repeat to make another chocolate bow. Place both on the cake using dabs of buttercream to secure them.

Make Sylvia's Trademark Glasses

Knead the black modeling chocolate until soft. Roll out a small section ¼ inch (6 mm) thick, and cut out two circles, two temples (the official name for the arms on glasses), and a small nose bridge. Use a tiny amount of water to "glue" the pieces together. Place the glasses at the bottom of the cake.

Make the Flowers

1. Roll a small bit of the gum paste into a ½-inch (12-mm) diameter sphere. Stretch the top of the ball until the entire shape resembles a teardrop. Stick a toothpick into the rounded bottom of the teardrop and stick the teardrop into the Styrofoam block and leave to set.

2. Lightly dust a flat surface with cornstarch. Roll out the gum paste $\frac{1}{16}$ inch (2 mm) thick. Cut out 6 rose petals shaped like fat teardrops, each about 2 inches (5 cm) wide. Take one petal, paint a little water on its lower half for adhesive, and wrap it around the teardrop. Take another petal and pinch the edges so they are thinner and slightly wavy. Paint a little water on it and wrap it around the previous petal, overlapping at the edges, and leaving it open at the top. Repeat with the remaining petals.

3. Make several more flowers in various sizes and in various stages of bloom: some wide open and some more closed. On Sylvia's cake, there are 5 large roses and 20 smaller ones.

4. Color a scoop of gum paste a very light green, and roll it out $\frac{1}{16}$ inch (2 mm) thick. Cut out leaves, then use a sharp knife to score veins on them. Roll floral wire in green gum paste and attach to the leaves. Arrange all of the flowers and leaves into a cascading bouquet at the top of the cake.

3, 2, 1 . . . Ya' done!

Tori, a senior care associate from Humble, Texas, not only appeared on two episodes, she won them both! Along the way, she charmed us with her infectious laugh, her dance-party energy, and the amazing way she rechristened fondant as "FUNdant."

Baker Spotlight:

KNEPHAUNATORIA "TORI" SMITH

Season 2, Episode 4, "Holi-Daze" and Nailed It! Holiday! Season 1, Episode 6, "3 . . . 2 . . . 1, Ya Done!"

▶ **What was the best thing about being on *Nailed It!*?**

The day they called and told me I was chosen, I hollered at the top of my lungs. It was one of the happiest days of my life! Once in LA, we were chauffeured to our hotel rooms and the studio. That made me feel like a celebrity and kept a smile on my face. Being surrounded by cameras and meeting the celebrity judges and Nicole was a dream come true, but I was soooooo nervous!

The second time, I knew what to expect, so I was able to relax more and truly enjoy the experience. When the driver picked me up from the airport, Sal [Venturelli] was in the van—my mouth dropped! I'm a HUGE fan of Sal. Meeting [the other contestants] along with seeing my crew (who made me feel like a celebrity again) was a real treat!

▶ **Any behind-the-scenes secrets you can share?**

We ate *real* good on the set! The crew that took care of us know what hospitality really is.

▶ **What's your favorite thing to bake?**

I just love to bake! It doesn't matter what it is. Cakes, pies, cookies (not the ones with the icing . . . watch the show and you'll know why)—anything that goes in the oven.

▶ **Any advice for home bakers, especially those who aren't great at it?**

Keep at it! You may not be the best yet, but with practice, you'll get there. And watching *Nailed It!* will help too. I almost won the cookie round the second time because I learned from the previous episode not to ice a hot cookie.

DONKEY PIÑATA CAKE

¡Nailed It! México. Season 1. Episode 1. "Birthday Blunders"

Makes one 2-layer, candy-filled piñata cake

A combination of two traditional Mexican celebrations, this donkey piñata is made entirely of cake and contains a candy-filled chocolate egg inspired by *cascarones*, eggshells filled with confetti or toys.

FOR THE CAKE

2½ cups (315 g) all-purpose flour

2 teaspoons baking powder

1 teaspoon baking soda

¼ teaspoon salt

4 large eggs

2 cups (400 g) sugar

⅔ cup (150 g) unsalted butter, melted

1 teaspoon vanilla extract

1 cup (240 ml) whole milk

Pink food coloring

FOR THE BUTTERCREAM

4 cups (8 sticks/900 g) unsalted butter, room temperature, cut into chunks

16 cups (2 kg) powdered sugar

1 tablespoon vanilla extract

½ teaspoon salt

¼ cup (60 ml) whole milk

FOR THE CHOCOLATE EGG

4 ounces (115 g) chocolate candy melts

½ cup (84 g) M&M's or other wrapper-less candy

FOR THE DECORATIONS

Orange, pink, neon green, and neon blue food coloring

8 ounces (225 g) black fondant

4 ounces (115 g) pink fondant

2 ounces (55 g) blue fondant

2 ounces (55 g) white fondant

SPECIAL EQUIPMENT

Three 8½ by 4½-inch (21.5 by 11-cm) loaf pans

Chocolate egg mold, 4 to 5 inches (10 to 12.5 cm) tall

Food-safe paintbrush

One 8 by 4-inch (20 by 10-cm) cake board

5 wooden cake dowels, ¼ inch (6 mm) thick and 4 inches (10 cm) long

Hot glue gun and glue

Styrofoam base, at least 10 by 5 inches (25 by 12 cm) and ½ inch (12 mm) thick

Food-safe wrapping paper or foil

Toothpicks

4 piping bags

4 piping bag couplers

1 ruffle piping tip

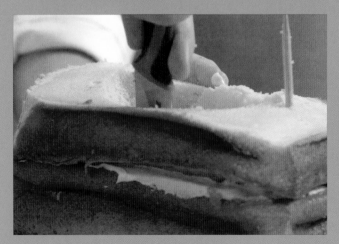

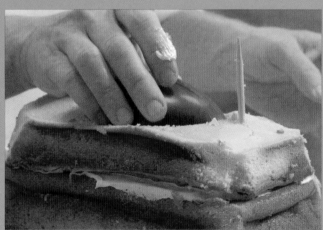

Make the Cake

1. Preheat the oven to 350°F (175°C). Grease the loaf pans. Cut three 8½ by 4½-inch (21.5 by 11-cm) pieces of parchment paper and place in the bottom of each pan.

2. In a large bowl, sift together the flour, baking powder, baking soda, and salt.

3. In another large bowl, using an electric mixer, combine the eggs, sugar, butter, vanilla, and milk. Add the dry mixture a large spoonful at a time and mix until just combined. Do not overmix. Use a spatula to scrape the sides and bottom of the bowl to incorporate the last bits of dry ingredients. Add a few drops of pink food coloring to the batter and stir to incorporate. Divide the batter among the pans, filling halfway.

4. Bake for 18 to 24 minutes, until a toothpick inserted in the center comes out clean. Let cool completely.

5. Run a butter knife around the edge of the pans. Place a plate over each pan and flip. Tap the bottom until the cakes slip out. Remove the parchment paper. If any of the cakes has a domed top, flip it over and cut it off with a large, serrated knife so the top is level. Set aside.

Make the Buttercream

1. We need a *lot* of buttercream for this recipe, and most mixers can't handle this much powdered sugar at one time, so we'll make it in four batches.

2. In a large bowl, using an electric mixer, beat 1 cup (2 sticks/225 g) of the butter until creamy, about 1 minute.

3. Add 4 cups (500 g) of the powdered sugar 1 cup (125 g) at a time, mixing until well combined.

4. Add 2 teaspoons of the vanilla, ⅛ teaspoon of the salt, and 2 tablespoons (30 ml) of the milk, and mix on high until thick and creamy. If the buttercream is too thin, add more powdered sugar, 1 tablespoon at a time. If the buttercream is too thick, add more milk, 1 tablespoon at a time.

5. Repeat with the remaining buttercream ingredients to make three more batches.

6. Scoop out 8 cups (1 kg) of white buttercream into a large glass bowl. Stir in a few drops of pink food coloring.

7. Fill three bowls each with 2½ cups (320 g) of buttercream. Color one bowl with orange food coloring, one with bright green, and one with bright blue.

Make the Chocolate Egg

1. Place the candy melts in a microwave-safe bowl. Microwave in 20-second bursts, stirring after each. When half melted, stir to melt the rest.

2. Spoon several scoops of the melted candy melts into each side of the egg mold. Swirl the mold so that the candy melt begins to cover the inside, then use a paintbrush to finish. Aim for a thick coating at least ¼ inch (6 mm) thick. Wipe down the edges of the mold so the eggs will have smooth sides to join to each other. Refrigerate until very firm, about 15 minutes. Gently pop each side of the egg out of its mold.

3. Carefully fill one side of the egg with M&M's. Zap the melted candy melts in the microwave for 10 seconds until soft again, then use to paint around the rim and press the other half of the egg on top.

PANIC

DON'T HAVE THREE LOAF PANS

You can easily make the recipe with just one pan in three shifts. Just make sure to completely cool the pan between baking.

Build the Cake Base

1. Wrap the Styrofoam base in food-safe wrapping paper or foil.

2. Take the cake board and cut four ¼-inch (6-mm) diameter holes into the corners for the feet, about 1½ inches (4 cm) from the shorter edges and ½ inch (12 mm) from the longer edges. Cut one more ¼-inch (6-mm) hole about 2 inches (5 cm) from the center of the short side on one end to support the head. (See diagram below.)

3. Stick four of the wooden dowels into the holes for the feet, leaving 1½ inches (4 cm) of the dowel above the cake board and 2½ inches (6 cm) below. Hot-glue the dowels into place. Stick the fifth wooden dowel into the hole for the head, leaving just ¼ inch (6 mm) beneath the cake board and the rest above. Hot-glue into place.

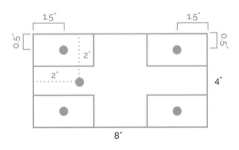

CAKE BOARD

Assemble the Cake

1. Set 2 of the cakes aside; they will be used for the donkey's body. The third remaining cake will be cut into pieces for the feet and head.

2. Place the third cake horizontally in front of you and slice a 1 by 4½-inch (2.5 by 11-cm) rectangle off the end. Cut that rectangle into 4 equal pieces; these will be the feet. Cut another 1 by 4½-inch (2.5 by 11-cm) strip off the cake, then cut two triangles from this strip and set them aside, discarding the excess; these triangles will be used for the ears. Set the remaining cake piece (which will be about 6½ by 4½ inches/16.5 by 11 cm) aside for the head.

3. Lay each donkey foot with the long cut side down (they should be about 2 to 3 inches/ 5 to 7.5 cm long, depending how deep the cake was before you cut it). One at a time, slide them fully onto the wooden dowels under the cake board, and then carefully press the exposed wooden dowels left poking out of the feet into the Styrofoam base.

4. Gently place one full cake layer onto the top of the cake board platform. Spread a layer of pink buttercream about ¼ inch (6 mm) thick on top and add the other full cake layer.

5. Carefully cut an egg-shaped hole out of the middle of the cake body and gently set the chocolate egg inside. Re-cover the hole with a thin piece of the cake you just cut out.

6. Cut the remaining rectangle reserved for the head in half so you have two pieces, each approximately 3¼ inches by 4½ inches (8 by 11 cm). Place one layer of the head over the fifth wooden dowel. Spread a thin layer of pink buttercream on top and add the second layer of the head. Add the ears to the top of the head, securing with buttercream and toothpicks.

7. Carefully frost the entire head and body with pink buttercream. It doesn't have to be smooth or pretty (as if you could have done that even if you wanted to), since we'll be covering it with ruffles.

Decorate!

1. Fit a piping bag with an icing coupler. Fill the bag with the remainder of the pink butter-cream. Prepare three more bags for the other icing colors.

2. Attach the piping tip to the bag of orange buttercream. Add ruffles around each leg until the legs are half covered. Move the piping tip to the pink buttercream and finish covering the legs in ruffles.

3. Attach the piping tip to the blue buttercream and pipe two layers of ruffles around the bottom of the donkey's body. Repeat with ruffles in green, then orange, then pink. Add colored ruffles around the donkey's head and on its back. Cover one ear in pink buttercream and one in blue.

4. Divide the black fondant in half. Lightly dust a flat surface with cornstarch. Roll out one piece ⅛ inch (3 mm) thick. Cut out 2 triangles for the inner ears. Stick onto the donkey's ears. Cut out four ½-inch (12-mm) circles. Attach 2 to the front of the donkey's head for nostrils. Set the other 2 black circles aside.

5. Roll the remaining black fondant into ropes a few inches (about 6 to 10 cm) long and attach to the back end of the donkey for its tail.

6. Roll out the white fondant ⅛ inch (3 mm) thick. Cut out two 1-inch (2.5-cm) circles. Cut out two ¼-inch (6-mm) circles. Cut out two ⅛-inch (3-mm) circles. Set aside.

7. Roll out the blue fondant ⅛ inch (3 mm) thick. Cut out two ¾-inch (2-cm) circles. Using a little water, attach the blue circles to the largest white circles for the eyes. Add the small black circles for pupils, then add the smallest white circles for sparkle.

8. Roll out the pink fondant ¼ inch (6 mm) thick for the bow on the tail. Cut out a 2 by 6-inch (5 by 15-cm) rectangle and a 1½ by ½-inch (40 by 12-mm) rectangle. Take the larger rectangle and fold the short ends back to make a loop. Gently squeeze the loop in the middle to form a bow. Wrap the smaller rectangle around the center to secure the bow. Place on the cake using a dab of buttercream to secure it.

3, 2, 1 . . . Ya' done!

PRINCESS TOWER CAKE

Season 1, Episode 2, "Fantasyland"

Makes one giant 8-layer tower cake

In this fantastical creation, Rapunzel waits in her tower surrounded by crispy rice cereal boulders. The knight, dragon, princess, and her glorious hair are all made from fondant—lots and lots of fondant. To stop this tallest-of-cakes from tumbling down, don't skip the internal support steps or you'll definitely be setting yourself up to fail it.

FOR THE CAKE

7½ cups (875 g) all-purpose flour

2 tablespoons baking powder

1 tablespoon baking soda

1 teaspoon salt

12 large eggs

6 cups (1.2 kg) sugar

3 cups (720 ml) whole milk

2¼ cups (540 ml) vegetable oil

1 tablespoon vanilla extract

FOR THE BUTTERCREAM

1 cup (2 sticks/225 g) unsalted butter, softened

4 cups (500 g) powdered sugar

2 teaspoons vanilla extract

⅛ teaspoon salt

¼ cup (60 ml) whole milk

FOR THE RICE CEREAL BOULDERS

5 tablespoons (68 g) unsalted butter

3¾ cups (188 g) mini marshmallows

5 cups (75 g) crispy rice cereal

FOR THE DECORATIONS

Green and pink food coloring

10 pounds (4.5 kg) gray fondant

24 ounces (680 g) white fondant

24 ounces (680 g) green fondant

8 ounces (225 g) yellow fondant

8 ounces (225 g) red fondant

4 ounces (115 g) brown fondant

2 ounces (55 g) skin-colored fondant

1 ounce (28 g) eye-colored fondant

Cornstarch

Edible gold paint

Edible silver paint

SPECIAL EQUIPMENT

Four 7-inch (17-cm) round cake pans

Four 6-inch (15-cm) round cake pans

Cake base or three 12-inch (30.5-cm) cake boards taped together and wrapped in foil

One 6-inch (15-cm) cake board

One 4-inch (10-cm) cake board

10 cake dowel rods

Food-safe paintbrush

Toothpicks

Make the Cake

1. Since most kitchen mixers can't accommodate the batter for eight cakes at once, we're going to split the job in half.

2. Preheat the oven to 350°F (175°C). Grease the cake pans. Cut out a circle of parchment paper for each pan and place in the bottom of each pan.

3. In a large bowl, sift together 3¾ cups (438 g) of the flour, 1 tablespoon of the baking powder, 1½ teaspoons of the baking soda, and ½ teaspoon of the salt.

4. In another large bowl, using an electric mixer, combine 6 of the eggs, 3 cups (600 g) of the sugar, 1½ cups (360 ml) of the milk, 1 cup plus 2 tablespoons (270 ml) of the vegetable oil, and 1½ teaspoons of the vanilla. Add the dry mixture a large spoonful at a time and mix until just combined. Do not overmix. Use a spatula to scrape the sides and bottom of the bowl to incorporate the last bits of dry ingredients. Divide the batter among two 7-inch (17-cm) pans and two 6-inch (15-cm) pans, filling halfway.

5. Repeat with the remaining cake ingredients, dividing the batter among the remaining four cake pans, filling halfway.

6. Bake for 20 to 28 minutes, until a toothpick inserted in the center comes out clean. Let cool.

Make the Buttercream

1. In a large bowl, using an electric mixer, beat the butter until creamy, about 1 minute.

2. Add the powdered sugar 1 cup (125 g) at a time, mixing until well combined.

3. Add the vanilla, salt, and milk, and mix on high until thick and creamy. If the buttercream is too thin, add more powdered sugar, 1 tablespoon at a time. If the buttercream is too thick, add more milk, 1 tablespoon at a time.

4. Add a few drops of pink food coloring to dye the buttercream. Set 1 cup (240 ml) of buttercream aside for piping flowers.

> **FROSTED TIP**
>
> To keep the crispy rice cereal mixture from sticking to your hands, spray your hands with cooking spray.

Create the Rice Cereal Shapes

1. In a large nonstick pot over medium-low, melt the butter.

2. Add the marshmallows and immediately take the pot off the heat. Stir continuously until the marshmallows are melted. Stir in the rice cereal and mix until coated. Pour the mixture onto a piece of parchment or foil on a flat surface.

3. When cool enough to handle, but not yet cold or too hard, scoop up a handful of the mixture and form it into a cone with a 4-inch (10-cm) base. Form the rest of the cereal mixture into various-size boulders, from 2 to 4 inches (5 to 10 cm) in diameter.

4. Cut a ¼-inch (6-mm) circle in the center of the 4-inch (10-cm) cake board. Using a dab of buttercream, secure the cone to the cake board. Stick a wooden dowel up through the hole and into the cone, leaving a few inches of dowel exposed under the cake board. Set aside.

Assemble the Cake

1. Place a dab of buttercream on the center of the cake base.

2. Run a butter knife around the edge of one of the 7-inch (17-cm) cake pans. Place a plate over the pan and flip. Tap the bottom until the cake slips out. Remove the parchment paper. If the cake has a domed top, flip it over and cut it off with a large, serrated knife so the top is level. Set the cake on the center of the cake base. Spread a thin layer of buttercream on top. Repeat with the remaining three 7-inch (17-cm) cakes. Coat the entire tier with a light layer of buttercream; it doesn't have to be smooth or pretty since it will be covered with fondant later.

3. Lightly set the 6-inch (15-cm) cake board on top of the cake stack and trace its outline with a knife or toothpick so you know where it will go. Remove the cake board. Hold a dowel next to the cake and mark the height on the dowel. Subtract ½ inch (12 mm) and cut five dowels to that length. Press the dowels into the cake, one in the center and the other four spaced out for support, but staying at least ½ inch (12 mm) inside the traced circle.

4. Arrange crispy rice cereal boulders around the base of the cake, molding them together with your hands and pushing them gently into the sides of the cake.

5. Lightly dust a large, flat surface with cornstarch. Roll out enough gray fondant to make a 30-inch (76-cm) circle ⅛ inch (3 mm) thick. Carefully lift and drape it over the cake tier and the boulders. Smooth the fondant with your hands and trim any excess.

6. Place the 6-inch (15-cm) cake board on a flat surface and put a dab of buttercream on the center. Remove one of the 6-inch (15-cm) cakes from its pan and set it on the center of the cake base. Spread a thin layer of buttercream on top. Repeat with the remaining 6-inch (15-cm) cakes.

7. Hold a dowel next to this cake tier and mark the height on the dowel. Subtract ½ inch (12 mm) and cut four dowels to that length. Press the dowels into the cake, spacing them out evenly. Cover the entire tier with buttercream.

8. Lightly re-dust the surface with cornstarch. Roll out enough gray fondant to make a 25-inch (63.5-cm) circle ⅛ inch (3 mm) thick. Carefully lift and drape it over the cake tier. Smooth the fondant with your hands and trim any excess. Put a dab of buttercream on top of the fondant-covered first tier and set this tier on top of it. Put another dab of buttercream on the top of the smaller tier and attach the rice cereal cone to it, sticking the wooden dowel down into the cake below for support.

PANIC

DON'T HAVE ENOUGH CAKE PANS

You can easily make the recipe with just one of each size pan. Just make sure to completely cool the pan between baking.

Decorate the Tower

1. Take a tennis ball–size scoop of the white fondant, add several drops of green food coloring, and knead it until the color is mixed throughout to create a very pale green. Lightly dust a flat surface with cornstarch. Roll out the fondant ⅛ inch (3 mm) thick. Rip this into large and small swaths of fondant to make moss to cover the castle tower. Attach by slightly wetting the back of the fondant with either the tip of your finger or a paintbrush dipped in water.

2. Roll out a section of gray fondant ⅛ inch (3 mm) thick. Cut out 35 squares, each ¾ inch (2 cm) wide. Cut out 25 squares, each ½ inch (12 mm) wide. Secure the large squares at intervals around the top of each cake tier to make turret bricks. Attach the small squares randomly onto the tower walls.

3. Using the packaged green fondant, roll several bushes and stick them around the base of the tower on top of the boulders, securing them with toothpicks. Use the rest of the green fondant to roll long ropes and attach to the tower as climbing vines.

4. Cover the rice cereal tower top with a thin layer of buttercream. Take a golf ball–size scoop of the white fondant, add a few drops of pink food coloring, and knead it until the color is mixed throughout. Repeat to make pale purple fondant. Roll out both colors of fondant ⅛ inch (3 mm) thick and cut enough ½-inch (12-mm) squares to cover the roof of the tower, alternating colors.

5. Use a pinch of white fondant to sculpt the ornament at the top of the tower. Stick it onto a toothpick, paint it gold, and when dry, stick into the top of the tower.

6. Roll out the brown fondant ⅛ inch (3 mm) thick and cut it to create a window frame. Attach it to the tower.

7. Use the skin-colored fondant to sculpt the princess's face. Use a toothpick or fondant tool to carve out her facial features. Attach in the window of the tower, securing with a toothpick. Use the eye color fondant to make small circles for the princess's eyes. Attach the eyes to her face with a drop of water.

8. Roll the yellow fondant into long ropes and attach them to the princess's face for her hair. Wind it down and around the tower walls.

9. Use gray or white fondant to sculpt the knight. Paint him silver and attach him to the base of the cake with toothpicks.

10. Use the red fondant to sculpt the dragon. Secure him to a boulder using toothpicks.

11. Put the reserved pink buttercream in a piping bag and pipe flowers all over the vines and moss on the tower.

3, 2, 1 . . . Ya' done!

TOY ROBOT CAKE

Nailed It! Holiday! Season 1, Episode 5, "Toying Around"

Makes one 4-layer cake

Beep-beep-boop-boop! Perhaps the most famous creation from *Nailed It!*, the toy robot is a four-layer, sweet red velvet cake with a head and arms sculpted from crispy rice cereal, covered in silver fondant, and featuring red and green eyes. It's also a joy to attempt because no matter how it ends up looking, it tastes delicious! This version of the recipe was adapted by Red Velvet NYC for the *Nailed It! At Home Experience* produced by Netflix and Fever, so it's a bit easier to create in your home kitchen than the gigantic version our contestants attempted on the show, which makes it a perfect option to bake for your own holiday celebrations.

FOR THE CAKE

1⅓ cups (175 g) cake flour

1½ tablespoons unsweetened cocoa

½ teaspoon salt

1 cup (200 g) sugar

⅔ cup (165 ml) vegetable oil

2 large eggs

1 teaspoon red food coloring

½ cup (120 ml) buttermilk

1 teaspoon baking soda

1 teaspoon white vinegar

FOR THE BUTTERCREAM

1 cup (2 sticks/225 g) unsalted butter, room temperature, cut into chunks

4 cups (500 g) powdered sugar

2 teaspoons vanilla extract

⅛ teaspoon salt

2 tablespoons (30 ml) whole milk

FOR THE RICE CEREAL ROBOT PARTS

1 tablespoon unsalted butter, softened

1½ cups (75 g) mini marshmallows

2 cups (30 g) crispy rice cereal

FOR THE DECORATIONS

2 tablespoons cornstarch

12 ounces (338 g) silver fondant

Jolly Ranchers

Spiced gumdrops

Gold M&M's

SPECIAL EQUIPMENT

9 by 13-inch (23 by 33-cm) baking pan

2 lollipop sticks

Sifter

Make the Cake

1. Preheat the oven to 350°F (175°C). Grease the pan.

2. In a medium bowl, sift together the cake flour, cocoa, and salt.

3. In a large bowl, using an electric mixer on medium speed, beat the sugar and oil until combined. Add the eggs and red food coloring, scraping down sides to incorporate fully. Reduce the speed to low. Add the dry mixture and buttermilk, alternating, until fully mixed. Use a spatula to scrape the sides and bottom of the bowl to incorporate the last bits of dry ingredients.

4. In a small bowl, combine the baking soda and vinegar (it will bubble and foam!). Add this to the batter and mix to combine.

5. Pour the batter into the pan and bake for 20 to 23 minutes, until a toothpick inserted in the center comes out clean. Let cool.

Make the Buttercream

1. In a large bowl, using an electric mixer, beat the butter until creamy, about 1 minute.

2. Add the powdered sugar 1 cup (125 g) at a time, mixing until well combined.

3. Add the vanilla, salt, and milk, and mix on high until thick and creamy. If the buttercream is too thin, add more powdered sugar, 1 tablespoon at a time. If the buttercream is too thick, add more milk, 1 tablespoon at a time.

Assemble the Cake

1. Remove the cake from the pan. Slice it up as follows: one 2-inch (5-cm) piece the length of the cake, and four equal squares from the remainder. Cut out the robot's feet from the long piece (see the photo on the left).

2. Place one square on a serving dish and top with a layer of buttercream. Place another square on top, and repeat, until all of the squares are stacked. Cover the entire cake in buttercream. You'll use about one-third of the buttercream between the layers, then another third to coat the outside. Save the remaining third in the refrigerator to use later.

Make the Body Parts

1. In a medium nonstick pot over medium-low, melt the butter.

2. Add the marshmallows and immediately take the pot off the heat. Stir continuously until the marshmallows melt. Stir in the rice cereal and mix until coated. Pour the mixture onto a piece of parchment or foil on a flat surface and allow to cool.

3. When cool enough to handle, but not yet cold or too hard, mold the mixture into a head, neck, arms, hands, and legs. Tip: The head should measure about 3 inches (7.5 cm) and arms about 4 inches (10 cm).

DON'T HAVE BUTTERMILK

PANIC

You can make your own! Simply add 1 tablespoon white vinegar or lemon juice to ½ cup (120 ml) whole milk. Stir to combine and let stand for 10 to 15 minutes, until the mixture begins curdling.

Make the Robot Features

1. Lightly dust a flat surface with cornstarch. Roll out the fondant thin enough so that you can cover the entire robot (about 1⁄16 inch/2 mm thick, the same thickness as a US quarter). Use a ruler to measure your cake and cut fondant panels to cover the chest, feet, arms, hands, head, and neck.

2. Cut out 50 bolts for the body, 12 for the head, and 16 for the feet.

3. Gather the scraps and roll them into coils for the neck; create a mouth, teeth, and a nose.

4. Apply the fondant panels to the robot's body, gently pressing them into the frosted cake. Use a drop of water or reserved buttercream to "glue" the bolts and other details to the panels.

5. Grease two tiny round metal cookie cutters or make squished rings from aluminum foil and place them on parchment on a cookie sheet. Take the Jolly Rancher candies out of their wrappers and crush them. Sprinkle the candy pieces into the rings, separating them by color. Bake at 300 for 5 minutes, or until the candy is melted. Remove from the oven and let cool completely before popping from the cutters. Use these candy circles for the robot's eyes, slicing them down to size if needed.

6. Using two lollipop sticks with spiced gumdrops on the ends, make a pair of antennae. If you're feeling fancy, you can wrap the lollipop sticks in a bit of extra fondant rolled very thin. Stick gold M&M's on the chest panel using reserved buttercream as "glue."

3, 2, 1 . . . Ya' done!

FROSTED TIP

Red velvet cake isn't just chocolate cake with red food coloring. It has a buttermilk and vinegar combination that makes the flavor richer.

SUSHI BOARD CAKE

Season 1, Episode 5, "Big in Japan"

Makes 6 small cakes

Impress your friends with these five oversize maki rolls and one huge salmon nigiri sushi—all made from cake! The salmon sushi is a white vanilla cake topped with jelly beans, the maki rolls are constructed from jelly-rolled chocolate coffee cake, and the side of ginger and wasabi are edible fondant.

FOR THE SUSHI CAKE

¾ cup (95 g) all-purpose flour

¼ teaspoon baking powder

¼ teaspoon baking soda

¼ teaspoon salt

1 large egg

⅓ cup (65 g) sugar

¼ cup (60 ml) vegetable oil

½ teaspoon vanilla extract

⅓ cup (80 ml) whole milk

FOR THE MAKI CAKES

8 large eggs, room temperature

½ cup plus 2 tablespoons (80 g) all-purpose flour

½ cup (50 g) unsweetened Dutch-process cocoa

1 teaspoon baking powder

½ teaspoon salt

1 cup (200 g) sugar

1 teaspoon instant coffee

FOR THE BUTTERCREAM

1 cup (2 sticks/225 g) unsalted butter, softened

4 cups (500 g) powdered sugar

2 teaspoons vanilla extract

⅛ teaspoon salt

¼ cup (60 ml) whole milk

FOR THE DECORATIONS

3 cups (550 g) white jelly beans

About 10 to 15 red jelly beans

8 ounces (225 g) white fondant

Red, orange, green, and black food coloring

1 cup (240 ml) ginger or peach jam

Cornstarch

Four strips of crispy bread

Various candies

SPECIAL EQUIPMENT

Approximately 5-inch (12-cm) oven-safe ramekin

13 by 18-inch (33 by 46-cm) half-sheet baking pan

Large wooden cutting board

Make the Sushi Cake

1. Preheat the oven to 350°F (175°C). (That's right, folks, this is sushi you make in the oven. Now you've seen everything, huh?) Grease the ramekin. Place it on a baking sheet.

2. In a medium bowl, sift together the flour, baking powder, baking soda, and salt.

3. In another medium bowl, using an electric mixer or whisk, beat the egg on high speed for 1 minute. Add the sugar and mix for 5 minutes. Add the vegetable oil and vanilla and mix until the batter is smooth, about 1 minute. Reduce the speed to low and alternate adding the flour mixture and the milk, beating until just combined. Use a spatula to scrape the sides and bottom of the bowl to incorporate the last bits of dry ingredients.

4. Pour the batter into the ramekin and bake for 18 to 25 minutes, until the top is golden brown and a toothpick inserted into the center comes out clean. Let cool.

Make the Maki Cake

1. If it isn't already, preheat the oven to 350°F (175°C). Grease the half-sheet baking pan with butter and line with parchment paper.

2. Separate the eggs, combining the whites in one bowl and the yolks in another.

3. In a medium bowl, sift together the flour, cocoa, baking powder, and salt. Set aside.

4. In a stand mixer with the whisk attachment, beat the egg yolks and ½ cup (100 g) of the sugar on high speed for 3 to 5 minutes until well combined.

5. In a small bowl, combine the instant coffee with 1 teaspoon water to dissolve. Add to the egg yolk mixture and whisk to combine. Transfer to another large bowl.

6. Clean and dry the stand mixer bowl and whisk attachment thoroughly, then transfer the egg whites to the bowl and beat on high speed until frothy. Gradually add the remaining sugar and beat until stiff peaks form. Gently fold the egg whites into the egg yolk mixture. Fold the dry ingredients into the egg mixture.

7. Pour the batter into the prepared tray. Bake for 15 minutes, until the cake springs back when touched in the center. Remove and let the cake cool in the pan for 10 minutes.

8. Generously dust a fresh piece of parchment paper with powdered sugar and turn the cake out onto it. Gently remove the old parchment paper from the bottom of the cake. Flip the edge of the parchment paper up and over the short side of the cake and begin rolling it with the parchment paper in the middle. Set the rolled cake aside.

Make the Buttercream

1. In a large bowl, using an electric mixer, beat the butter until creamy, about 1 minute.

2. Add the powdered sugar 1 cup (125 g) at a time, mixing until well combined.

3. Add the vanilla, salt, and milk, and mix on high until thick and creamy. If the buttercream is too thin, add more powdered sugar, 1 tablespoon at a time. If the buttercream is too thick, add more milk, 1 tablespoon at a time.

Assemble the Sushi Cake

1. Remove the cooled sushi cake from its pan and carve into a large bean shape. Cover with a layer of buttercream.

2. Press white jelly beans all over the buttercream.

3. Take a pinch of white fondant and use orange food coloring to color it orange. Roll it into 6 thick ropes 2 inches (5 cm) long. Roll a pinch of white fondant into 6 thick ropes 2 inches (5 cm) long. Set the ropes side by side, alternating colors, on a flat surface, then roll with a rolling pin to form the striped piece for the salmon. Cut any ragged edges off to create a rectangle with slightly rounded corners and set it on top of the sushi cake. Place on your cutting board for presentation.

Assemble the Maki Rolls

1. Gently unroll the cooled maki cake and remove the parchment paper. Spread a thin layer of jam onto the cake. Top with a thin layer of buttercream. Tightly roll the cake back up. Wrap in plastic wrap and refrigerate for 10 minutes.

2. Color a pinch of the fondant orange and another pinch green. Color the remaining fondant black.

3. Lightly dust a flat surface with cornstarch. Roll out the black fondant until ⅛ inch (3 mm) thick.

4. Remove the jelly roll from the refrigerator and cut it into 5 equal pieces (each will be about 2½ inches/6 cm long). Trim all edges so they are straight. Cut 5 strips, each 3½ inches (9 cm) wide, out of the black fondant. Wrap a piece of cake in a strip of black fondant so that the cake is even with one side, but the fondant extends 1 inch (2.5 cm) past the top of the cake. Stand the pieces up and trim any excess, leaving a 1-inch (2.5-cm) deep cup at the top to fill in the next step.

Decorate!

1. Fill the tops of the maki rolls with white jelly beans for rice and decorate with strips of bread and the various candy pieces, using the photo on page 102 as a reference. Set on a presentation board.

2. Roll out the orange fondant ¹⁄₁₆ inch (2 mm) thick. Lift it up and gently crumple it into a loose ball to make the pickled ginger. Set on the board.

3. Form the green fondant into a lumpy ball for the wasabi and place on the board.

3, 2, 1 . . . Ya' done!

GRANDMA COOKIE CAKE

Nailed It! Double Trouble Episode 5. "I've Failed and I Can't Get Up"

Makes one 9-layer cake and 12 chocolate chip cookies

The grandmother of all cakes, this nine-layer cake is also a working cookie jar, complete with Nana's favorite chocolate chip cookies. This ultimate challenge includes homemade cake, cookies, buttercream, crispy rice cereal treats, fondant, modeling chocolate, and edible glaze to make the whole thing look like ceramic.

FOR THE CAKE

10 cups (1.2 kg) all-purpose flour

8 teaspoons baking powder

4 teaspoons baking soda

2 teaspoons salt

16 large eggs

8 cups (1.6 kg) sugar

3 cups (6 sticks/675 g) unsalted butter

4 teaspoons vanilla extract

4 cups (960 ml) whole milk

FOR THE COOKIES

1¼ cups (155 g) all-purpose flour

½ cup (110 g) brown sugar

¼ cup (50 g) granulated sugar

½ cup (1 stick/115 g) unsalted butter, melted

½ teaspoon baking soda

½ teaspoon salt

1 large egg

1 teaspoon vanilla extract

1 cup (175 g) chocolate chips

FOR THE BUTTERCREAM

2 cups (4 sticks/450 g) unsalted butter, softened

8 cups (1 kg) powdered sugar

4 teaspoons vanilla extract

¼ teaspoon salt

½ cup (120 ml) whole milk

FOR THE RICE CEREAL TOP

5 tablespoons (68 g) unsalted butter

3¾ cups (188 g) mini marshmallows

5 cups (75 g) crispy rice cereal

FOR THE DECORATIONS

24 ounces (680 g) blue fondant

12 ounces (340 g) white fondant

2 pounds (910 g) white modeling chocolate

Shortening

Yellow, pink, brown, gray, black, and skin-colored food coloring

Edible glaze spray, one small can (these often come in size 3.4 ounces/100 ml)

(continued on page 111)

SPECIAL EQUIPMENT

Three 10-inch (25-cm) round cake pans

Three 8-inch (20-cm) round cake pans

Three 6-inch (15-cm) round cake pans

Cookie sheet

One 8-inch (20-cm) round cake board

Three 6-inch (15-cm) round cake boards

¾-inch (2-cm) diameter PVC pipe rated for drinking water, 9 inches (23 cm) long

One ¾ by ½-inch (20 by 12-mm) PVC slip-reducing bushing

Spade drill bit, ¾ inch (2 cm) diameter

14-inch (35.5-cm) round MDF wooden board

Foil or food-safe paper

Hot glue gun and glue

Two 9-inch (23-cm) pieces of 18-gauge food-safe floral or cake wire

Toothpicks

Food-safe paintbrush

Build the Cake Armature

1. Building cake armature out of PVC pipe is one of the quickest, easiest, and most inexpensive methods; just make sure to get PVC pipe that's rated for drinking water since it's food safe (but wash it well before using it!).

2. Cut off the smaller end of PVC bushing so that it will slide completely onto the PVC pipe. (You can cut it with a PVC cutter, or a hacksaw, or ask an employee at the hardware store where you buy it to cut it for you.) Set aside. When we push the bushing onto the pipe later, it should be an extremely snug fit.

3. Mark the center of the MDF board and drill a ¾-inch (2-cm) hole three-quarters of the way deep (not all the way through). Cover the MDF board with foil or food-safe paper, leaving the hole open, to make the cake base. Line the inside of the hole with hot glue. Insert the PVC pipe. Allow to set.

4. Cut a ¾-inch (2-cm) hole in the center of each of the cake boards. Set aside.

Make the Cake

1. Since most kitchen mixers can't accommodate the batter for a cake this large, we're going to quarter the recipe and make it four times.

2. Preheat the oven to 350°F (175°C). Grease the cake pans. Cut out a circle of parchment paper for each pan and place in the bottom of each pan.

3. In a large bowl, sift together 2½ cups (315 g) of the flour, 2 teaspoons of the baking powder, 1 teaspoon of the baking soda, and ½ teaspoon of the salt.

4. In another large bowl, using an electric mixer, combine 4 of the eggs, 2 cups (400 g) of the sugar, ¾ cup (1½ sticks/370 g) of the butter, 1 teaspoon of the vanilla, and 1 cup (240 ml) of the milk. Add the dry mixture a large spoonful at a time and mix until just combined. Do not overmix. Use a spatula to scrape the sides and bottom of the bowl to incorporate the last bits of dry ingredients.

5. Pour the batter into one 10-inch (25-cm) and one 8-inch (20-cm) pan, filling halfway, and bake for 24 to 28 minutes, until a toothpick inserted in the center comes out clean. Let cool.

6. Repeat steps 1 through 4 three more times to make a total of three 10-inch (25-cm) cakes, three 8-inch (20-cm) cakes, and three 6-inch (15-cm) cakes.

Make the Cookies

1. Preheat the oven to 350°F (175°C). Line the cookie sheet with parchment paper.

2. In a large bowl, sift together the flour, brown sugar, granulated sugar, butter, baking soda, and salt and stir until combined. Add the egg and vanilla and mix until combined. Stir in the chocolate chips to distribute evenly throughout the dough.

3. Shape the dough into 12 equally sized balls and place on the baking sheet. Bake for 8 to 12 minutes, until the edges are just set and the tops are golden brown. Let cool.

Make the Buttercream

1. We need a *lot* of buttercream for this recipe, and most mixers can't handle this much powdered sugar at one time, so we'll make it in two batches.

2. In a large bowl, using an electric mixer, beat 1 cup (2 sticks/225 g) of the butter until creamy, about 1 minute.

3. Add 4 cups (500 g) of the powdered sugar 1 cup (125 g) at a time, mixing until well combined.

4. Add 2 teaspoons of the vanilla, ⅛ teaspoon of the salt, and ¼ cup (60 ml) of the milk, and mix on high until thick and creamy. If the buttercream is too thin, add more powdered sugar, 1 tablespoon at a time. If the buttercream is too thick, add more milk, 1 tablespoon at a time.

5. Repeat with the remaining buttercream ingredients to make a second batch.

Assemble the Cake

1. Place a dab of buttercream on the 10-inch (25-cm) cake base.

2. Run a butter knife around the edge of one of the 10-inch (25-cm) cake pans. Place a plate over the pan and flip. Tap the bottom until the cake slips out. Remove the parchment paper. If the cake has a domed top, flip it over and cut it off with a large, serrated knife so the top is level. Set the cake on the 10-inch (25-cm) cake base. Cut a ¾-inch (2-cm) hole in the center of the cake and remove the excess cake. With a spatula (an offset spatula works great if you have one), spread a layer of buttercream on top, leaving the hole open. Repeat with the remaining 10-inch (25-cm) cakes.

3. Carefully lift the 10-inch (25-cm) tier and slide it over the cake armature pipe to rest on the cake base.

4. Repeat steps 1–2 for the 8-inch (20-cm) cakes.

5. Repeat steps 1–2 for the 6-inch (15-cm) cakes.

6. Using a serrated knife, carve the lower cake into a rounded shape for Grandma's lower body, the middle tier into Grandma's upper body, and the top tier into her head, using the photo as a reference.

7. Slice the top of the top tier off so the cake has a flat surface, then carve out a hole 2 inches (5 cm) deep for storing cookies later.

Create the Rice Cereal Lid

1. In a large nonstick pot over medium-low, melt the butter.

2. Add the marshmallows and immediately take the pot off the heat. Stir continuously until the marshmallows melt. Stir in the rice cereal and mix until coated. Pour the mixture onto a piece of parchment or foil on a flat surface and allow to cool.

3. When cool enough to handle, but not yet cold or too hard, scoop up a handful of the mixture and form it into the top of the cookie jar, using the photos as a reference. Grandma's hair should be at least 7 inches (17 cm) across. Set aside.

Cover the Cake Body in Fondant

1. Cover the entire cake with a layer of buttercream. It doesn't have to be pretty or smooth because we'll be covering it with fondant. Do not frost the inside of the cookie jar.

2. Lightly dust a flat surface with cornstarch. Roll out the blue fondant into a large rectangle 32 by 10 inches (81 by 25 cm). Wrap it around the bottom tier of the cake and smooth with your hands. Roll out another blue fondant rectangle 26 by 8 inches (66 by 20 cm). Wrap it around the middle tier of the cake and smooth down. Trim any excess so the seams match. Mix a bit of the blue fondant on the palm of your hand with a dab of shortening and press into the seams to blend them together.

3. Roll out the white fondant to about ¼ inch (6 mm) thick and cut out Grandma's apron, collar, apron pockets, and a plate of cookies. Set the pockets and plate of cookies aside. Attach the apron and collar to the body using a bit of water on a paintbrush. Paint stripes on the white apron with pink food coloring.

Make the Head and Arms

1. Knead the white modeling chocolate until soft. Split it in half and color one half gray. Set the gray modeling chocolate aside.

2. Pull off 2 golf ball–size chunks of white modeling chocolate. Color one black and one pink and set aside. Pull off a tennis ball–size chunk of white modeling chocolate. Set it aside.

3. Split the remaining modeling chocolate in half. Color one half blue and the other skin colored.

4. Roll out the skin-colored modeling chocolate to around ¼ to ½ inch (7 to 12 mm) thick and wrap it around the top layer of the cake to make Grandma's face. Add more skin-colored modeling chocolate to make her nose, carving her features with a sharp knife and using the photo as a reference.

5. Roll out the white modeling chocolate and cut out two small eyes. Attach to the face using a dab of water on each.

6. Roll out the gray modeling chocolate. Cut out eyebrows and attach them above the eyes. Wrap gray chocolate around the cookie jar lid. Use a sharp knife or modeling tool to etch in hair texture.

7. Form the two cake wires into arms that will rest against Grandma's body. Use blue, white, and skin-colored modeling chocolate to sculpt the arms around the wires, just as you would with clay, leaving 1½ inches (4 cm) of wire free to secure them to the cake. Attach them to the cake.

Add Final Details

1. Make a tiny pink bow shape using the pink modeling chocolate. Attach it to Grandma's hair using a drop of water, securing with a short piece of toothpick if necessary.

2. Use the black modeling chocolate to form a very thin "wire" and shape it into square-framed glasses. Attach to Grandma's face using drops of water.

3. Make a pink and white oval-shaped brooch about ½ inch (12 mm) tall using modeling chocolate. Attach to front of Grandma's apron using drops of water.

4. Attach the fondant pockets and plate of cookies to the front of the apron using drops of water. Use food coloring to paint on colors and details. Use paint to fill in the eyes.

5. Once all the paint is dry, spray both the body and lid of the cookie jar with edible glaze spray. Allow to dry.

6. Place a few chocolate chip cookies inside the cookie jar, arranging the rest around the base of the jar. Top with the lid.

3, 2, 1 . . . Ya' done!

TUSKEGEE AIRMEN CAKE

Season 6. Episode 4. "History in the Baking"

Makes one 2-tier, 3-layer cake

This heroic cake honors the Tuskegee Airmen, the first Black military aviators in the United States Army Air Corps, who flew more than fifteen thousand missions during World War II. The cake is a rich chocolate layered with buttercream; the airplane is made of crispy rice cereal covered in modeling chocolate.

FOR THE CAKE

3 cups (375 g) all-purpose flour

¾ cup (70 g) unsweetened cocoa

1 tablespoon baking powder

1½ teaspoons baking soda

½ teaspoon salt

6 large eggs

3 cups (600 g) sugar

1½ cups (360 ml) whole milk

¾ cup (180 ml) vegetable oil

FOR THE BUTTERCREAM

1 cup (2 sticks/225 g) unsalted butter, softened

4 cups (500 g) powdered sugar

2 teaspoons vanilla extract

⅛ teaspoon salt

¼ cup (60 ml) whole milk

FOR THE RICE CEREAL PLANE

1 tablespoon butter

¾ cup (38 g) mini marshmallows

1 cup (15 g) crispy rice cereal

FOR THE DECORATIONS

Cornstarch

16 ounces (455 g) navy blue fondant

Edible glitter

16 ounces (455 g) yellow fondant

One 1½-ounce (45-ml) can color mist spray in brown, red, and orange

8 ounces (225 g) gray modeling chocolate

8 ounces (225 g) white modeling chocolate

Red, blue, and black food coloring

4 ounces (115 g) black fondant

4 ounces (115 g) red fondant

4 ounces (115 g) brown modeling chocolate

4 ounces (115 g) dark green modeling chocolate

2 ounces (55 g) your choice of skin-colored modeling chocolate

SPECIAL EQUIPMENT

One 10-inch (25-cm) round cake pan

Two 8-inch (20-cm) round cake pans

Cake base or three 12-inch (30.5-cm) cake boards stacked and taped together and wrapped in foil

One 8-inch (20-cm) cake board

3 cake dowel rods

Food-safe paintbrush

Food-safe floral or cake wire

Foil

Toothpicks

Make the Cake

1. Preheat the oven to 325°F (165°C). Grease the cake pans. Cut out a circle of parchment paper for each pan and place in the bottom of each pan.

2. In a large bowl, sift together the flour, cocoa, baking powder, baking soda, and salt.

3. In another large bowl, using an electric mixer, combine the eggs, sugar, milk, and oil. Add the dry mixture a large spoonful at a time and mix until just combined. Do not overmix. Use a spatula to scrape the sides and bottom of the bowl to incorporate the last bits of dry ingredients.

4. Pour the batter into the pans, filling halfway, and bake for 24 to 28 minutes, until a toothpick inserted in the center comes out clean. Let cool.

Make the Buttercream

1. In a large bowl, using an electric mixer, beat the butter until creamy, about 1 minute.

2. Add the powdered sugar 1 cup (125 g) at a time, mixing until well combined.

3. Add the vanilla, salt, and milk, and mix on high until thick and creamy. If the buttercream is too thin, add more powdered sugar, 1 tablespoon at a time. If the buttercream is too thick, add more milk, 1 tablespoon at a time.

Assemble the Bottom Cake

1. Place a dab of buttercream on the center of the cake base.

2. Run a butter knife around the edge of the 10-inch (25-cm) cake pan. Place a plate over the pan and flip. Tap the bottom until the cake slips out. Remove the parchment paper. If the cake has a domed top, flip it over and cut it off with a large, serrated knife so the top is level. Set the cake on the center of the cake base. Spread a layer of buttercream about ¼ to ½ inch (7 to 12 mm) thick on the top and sides of the cake; it doesn't have to be smooth since we'll be covering it with fondant later.

3. Lightly dust a large, flat surface with cornstarch. Roll out the navy blue fondant into a thin circle about ⅛ inch (3 mm) thick and large enough to cover the first layer of the cake. Drape it over the cake and smooth it down with your hands. Trim any excess from around the bottom.

4. Mix the edible glitter with 1 tablespoon water and paint over the fondant to give the outside of the cake a subtle sparkly effect. (Or, if your style is more like Nicole's, load up on the glitter for a not-so-subtle sparkly effect. It's your cake.)

Assemble the Top Cake

1. We're going to stack and cover this layer in fondant before we set it on top of the navy blue layer.

2. Place the 8-inch (20-cm) cake board on a flat surface and put a dab of buttercream in the center.

3. Run a butter knife around the edge of one of the 8-inch (20-cm) cake pans. Place a plate over the pan and flip. Tap the bottom until the cake slips out. Remove the parchment paper. Set the cake on the center of the cake base. If the cake has a domed top, cut it off with a large, serrated knife so the top is level. With a spatula (an offset spatula works great if you have one), spread a layer of buttercream on top. Repeat with the other 8-inch (20-cm) cake. Cover the entire tier with a layer of buttercream.

4. Lightly re-dust the surface with cornstarch. Roll out the yellow fondant into a thin sheet about ⅛ inch (3 mm) thick and large enough to cover the two-tier cake. Drape it over the cake and smooth it with your hands. Trim any excess from around the bottom.

5. Spray a band of brown color mist along the bottom of the cake. Spray a band of red above the brown, and then orange above the red, leaving a band of yellow at the top. Let dry.

6. Place a dab of buttercream on the center of the top of the navy blue cake. Carefully place the yellow cake on top of it.

Make the Airplane

1. In a small nonstick pot over medium-low, melt the butter.

2. Add the marshmallows and immediately take the pot off the heat. Stir continuously until the marshmallows melt. Stir in the rice cereal and mix until coated. Pour the mixture onto a piece of parchment or foil on a flat surface and allow to cool.

3. When cool enough to handle, but not yet cold or too hard, scoop the mixture up and form it into an airplane, using the photo as a reference. Stick a wooden cake dowel into the bottom of the airplane.

4. Knead the gray modeling chocolate until soft. Cover the airplane with the modeling chocolate, smoothing the edges. Color a pinch of white modeling chocolate blue. Color another red, and a smaller ball black. Use the colors to make the plane's cockpit, decorations, and propeller. Attach them to the plane with a little water as "glue."

5. Use the rest of the white modeling chocolate to form clouds. Attach them to the top of the cake using toothpicks.

6. Stick the plane on top of the cake in the middle of the clouds.

Make the Silhouettes and Slogan

1. Lightly dust a flat surface with cornstarch. Roll out the black fondant ⅛ inch (3 mm) thick. Cut out the silhouettes of 7 airmen, and with a tiny bit of water, attach them to the front of the top cake.

2. Roll out the red fondant ⅛ inch (3 mm) thick and cut out the Tuskegee Airmen logo. Attach it to the front of the bottom cake using a little water as "glue." Add white fondant stars.

Make the Airmen

1. Knead the skin-colored modeling chocolate until soft. Shape floral wire into the skeleton of an airman's arms and legs and cover with the modeling chocolate. Repeat for a second airman.

2. Crumple pieces of foil to make the heads and bodies.

3. Knead the brown modeling chocolate until soft. Make the airmen's jackets by pressing the modeling chocolate directly onto the foil and shaping it as necessary.

4. Knead the green modeling chocolate until soft, and use it to make the pants.

5. Cover the heads and necks with the skin-colored modeling chocolate. Use brown modeling chocolate to make their hats and boots. Use white modeling chocolate to add a shirt collar and eyes. Use black modeling chocolate to add goggles and pupils.

6. Use a toothpick to etch details into each airman. Set each airman on the bottom layer of the cake, securing them with the wooden dowels.

3, 2, 1 . . . Ya' done!

Baker Spotlight:
ALICIA FIGLIUOLO

Nailed It! Holiday! Season 1. Episode 5. "Toying Around"

Appearing on *Nailed It!* proved to Alicia, a United States Marine Corps veteran from New Braunfels, Texas, who had suffered a traumatic brain injury, that she could reclaim her passion for baking and a piece of herself. Her perseverance and hopeful attitude—she recently got a tattoo of the "Nightmare Dolly" cookie she created on her bicep—inspired thousands.

▶ **What has the fan reaction been like?**

I can say without a shadow of a doubt that *Nailed It!* has the greatest fans in the world. As soon as the season dropped, children started noticing me in public, wanting to take pictures, talk about Jacques and Nicole. I assumed it would cool down, and I would be a relic in streaming reality TV, but boy was I wrong! Even three years later, people from all over the world keep reaching out to me and telling me their stories of trauma, survival, and seeing themselves in me.

▶ **What did being on the show mean to you?**

Nailed It! changed my life. Up until the day of my physical for the show, my doctors were mum on my request to compete in a kitchen with sharp things and ovens. At this point, I wasn't allowed to drive, cook, or shower without someone in the area. I hadn't baked anything in almost a year. I made a pan of brownies for the audition video in a friend's kitchen and had to have my occupational therapist sign off that she believed I was ready to enter into a high-pressure situation like the *Nailed It!* kitchen. I was super excited to prove to myself that I was strong enough to compete, and I baked my heart out.

Nailed It! healed a section of my soul and gave me my independence back. I baked in a kitchen under extreme circumstances that pushed me beyond anything I had done up until that time with therapy. I executed two recipes that required finesse and strategic planning all while remembering the steps, the ingredients, and the presentation. I might not have won the competition, but I proved to myself that my brain was truly creating new neural pathways, and that I was going to be okay. I was going to be me again.

▶ **What was your favorite memory from filming?**

When the judges came to taste my "Nightmare Dolly" cookie, Jacques ate her little arm, Nicole took a bite of her, and [guest judge] Ron Funches snacked on a little piece. They all praised it. Ron and Nicole walked away, but Jacques stayed two steps behind, grabbed another piece, and said it tasted really good! Jacques Torres didn't spit out the first bite and hung back for a second one! I didn't need to win the competition; that was a win in my book.

▶ **Any behind-the-scenes secrets you want to share?**

Nicole is the freaking greatest human with a true soul of love. We were chatting during the cake round and talking about the military. Somehow, we started talking about push-ups and next thing I know, me, her, and a few production people are in front of my station doing full-blown Marine Corps–style push-ups. I stopped after three, washed my hands, and kept baking. I looked over at my station, and Nicole was still busting out push-ups, and the crew was in hysterics.

▶ **What's your favorite thing to bake?**

I love cupcakes and pucks! Cupcakes are three bites of perfection, and the flavor profiles are endless. Pucks are something I make from cake mixed with buttercream smashed into a puck mold and covered in chocolate or different types of candy melts. These little pucks are full of flavor and offer a fun flat space for decorating to your heart's content.

▶ **Any advice for home bakers, especially those who aren't great at it?**

Jacques Torres and every single baker in this world started out just like you and me: scared, excited, and unsure of their passion, but they kept going, kept creating, and are now doing what they love. Don't ever sell yourself short because you might miss out on some amazing experiences.

Baker Spotlight: Alicia Figliuolo

LOCH NESS MONSTER CAKE

Season 6, Episode 2, "Paranormal Pastries"

Makes one monstrous 4-layer cake

Scotland's shyest and most beloved mythical creature is celebrated in this magnificent, butterscotch-flavored cake. To support the legendary monster's rice cereal head, we'll need to first build some quick-and-easy armature (like a skeleton for cake) using PVC pipe. And just as visitors to Loch Ness must beware of monsters, bakers should beware of this monstrously complex challenge. We believe in you (well . . . some of us do), but regardless of how seaworthy—or not—your creature turns out, rest assured the butterscotch cake is delicious.

FOR THE CAKE

5 cups (625 g) all-purpose flour

4 teaspoons baking powder

2 teaspoons baking soda

1 teaspoon salt

8 large eggs

4 cups (800 g) sugar

1½ cups (3 sticks/340 g) unsalted butter

2 teaspoons butterscotch flavoring

2 cups (480 ml) whole milk

FOR THE BUTTERCREAM

2 cups (4 sticks/450 g) unsalted butter, softened

8 cups (1 kg) powdered sugar

4 teaspoons vanilla extract

¼ teaspoon salt

½ cup (120 ml) whole milk

FOR THE RICE CEREAL SHAPES

3 tablespoons unsalted butter

2¼ cups (113 g) mini marshmallows

3 cups (45 g) crispy rice cereal

FOR THE DECORATIONS

3 pounds (1.4 kg) dark green fondant

24 ounces (680 g) light green fondant

4 ounces (115 g) blue fondant

2 pounds (910 g) white modeling chocolate

18 ounces (510 g) brown modeling chocolate

Red, green, and black food coloring

(continued on page 122)

SPECIAL EQUIPMENT

Two 10-inch (25-cm) round cake pans

Two 8-inch (20-cm) round cake pans

One 4-inch (10-cm) round cake pan

One 10-inch (25-cm) round cake board

One 8-inch (20-cm) round cake board

Two 4-inch (10-cm) round cake boards

¾-inch (2-cm) diameter PVC pipe rated for drinking water, 18 inches (46 cm) long

One ¾ by ½-inch (20 by 12-mm) PVC slip-reducing bushing

Spade drill bit, ¾ inch (2 cm) diameter

14-inch (35.5-cm) diameter round MDF wooden board

Foil or food-safe paper

Hot glue gun and glue

Food-safe floral or cake wire, 18 gauge

Toothpicks

Food-safe paintbrush

Build the Cake Armature

1. This is one of the quickest, easiest, and most inexpensive ways to build your own cake armature. Make sure to get PVC pipe that's rated for drinking water, as it's considered food safe and doesn't need to be wrapped in foil (give it a good scrub before using it though!).

2. Cut off the smaller end of PVC bushing so that it will slide completely onto the PVC pipe. (You can cut it with a PVC cutter, or a hacksaw, or ask an employee at the hardware store where you buy it to cut it for you.) Set aside. When we push the bushing onto the pipe later, it should be an extremely snug fit.

3. Mark the center of the MDF board and drill a ¾-inch (2-cm) hole three-quarters of the way deep (not all the way through). Cover the MDF board with foil or food-safe paper, leaving the hole open, to make the cake base. Line the inside of the hole with hot glue. Insert the PVC pipe. Allow to set.

Make the Cake

1. Since most kitchen mixers can't accommodate the batter for a cake this large, we're going to split the job in half.

2. Preheat the oven to 350°F (175°C). Grease the cake pans. Cut out a circle of parchment paper for each pan and place in the bottom of each pan.

3. In a large bowl, sift together 2½ cups (312 g) of the flour, 2 teaspoons of the baking powder, 1 teaspoon of the baking soda, and ½ teaspoon of the salt.

4. In another large bowl, using an electric mixer, combine 4 of the eggs, 2 cups (400 g) of the sugar, ¾ cup (1½ sticks/170 g) of the butter, 1 teaspoon of the butterscotch flavoring, and 1 cup (240 ml) of the milk. Add the dry mixture a large spoonful at a time and mix until just combined. Do not overmix. Use a spatula to scrape the sides and bottom of the bowl to incorporate the last bits of dry ingredients.

5. Divide the batter between the two 10-inch (25-cm) pans, filling halfway, and bake for 24 to 28 minutes, until a toothpick inserted in the center comes out clean. Let cool.

6. Repeat with the remaining cake ingredients, dividing the batter among the remaining three cake pans.

> ## FROSTED TIP
>
> An easy way to pick up a large circle of fondant? Wrap it around a rolling pin!

Make the Buttercream

1. We need a *lot* of buttercream for this recipe, and most mixers can't handle this much powdered sugar at one time, so we'll make it in two batches.

2. In a large bowl, using an electric mixer, beat 1 cup (2 sticks/225 g) of the butter until creamy, about 1 minute.

3. Add 4 cups (500 g) of the powdered sugar 1 cup (125 g) at a time, mixing until well combined.

4. Add 2 teaspoons of the vanilla, ⅛ teaspoon of the salt, and ¼ cup (60 ml) of the milk, and mix on high until thick and creamy. If the buttercream is too thin, add more powdered sugar, 1 tablespoon at a time. If the buttercream is too thick, add more milk, 1 tablespoon at a time.

5. Repeat with the remaining buttercream ingredients to make a second batch.

Assemble the Cake Layers

1. Cut a ¾-inch (2-cm) hole into the center of the 10-inch (25-cm), 8-inch (20-cm), and one of the 4-inch (10-cm) cake boards.

2. Run a butter knife around the edge of one of the 10-inch (25-cm) cake pans. Place a plate over the pan and flip. Tap the bottom until the cake slips out. Remove the parchment paper. If the cake has a domed top, flip it over and cut it off with a large, serrated knife so the top is level. Set the cake on the 10-inch (25-cm) cake base. Cut a ¾-inch (2-cm) hole in the center of the cake and remove the excess cake. With a spatula (an offset spatula works great if you have one), spread a layer of buttercream on top, leaving the hole open. Repeat with the remaining 10-inch (25-cm) cake.

3. Using a serrated knife, shape the cake tier into a rounded shape, like a donut. (This will be the bottom coil of Nessie's body. See the photo for reference.) Cover the entire tier with a layer of buttercream. It doesn't have to be pretty or smooth because we'll be covering it with fondant later. Set aside.

4. Remove one of the 8-inch (20-cm) cakes from its pan, level if needed, and place it on the 8-inch (20-cm) cake board. Cut a ¾-inch (2-cm) hole in the center of the cake and remove the excess cake. With a spatula (an offset spatula works great if you have one), spread a layer of buttercream on top, leaving the hole open. Repeat with the remaining 8-inch (20-cm) cake.

5. Using a serrated knife, shape the cake tier into another rounded shape, like a donut. (This will be the next coil of Nessie's body. See the photo for reference.) Cover the entire tier with a layer of buttercream. Set aside.

6. Remove the 4-inch (10-cm) cake from its pan, level if needed, and place it on the 4-inch (10-cm) cake board. Cut a ¾-inch (2-cm) hole in the center of the cake and remove the excess cake. Shape the cake tier into a rounded shape, like a donut. Cover the entire tier with a layer of buttercream.

Cover the Cakes in Fondant

1. Lightly dust a flat surface with cornstarch. Roll out a piece of the dark green fondant into a thin sheet about ⅛ inch (3 mm) thick and large enough to cover the top half of the 10-inch (25-cm) cake tier (about 16 inches/40.5 cm in diameter). Drape it over the tier and smooth it with your hands. Trim the edges so the fondant only goes halfway down the sides. Cut a ¾-inch (2-cm) hole in the center of the fondant on top, aligning it with the hole in the cake tier.

2. Roll out a piece of the light green fondant into a rectangle 4 by 16 inches (10 by 40.5 cm). Cut it in half lengthwise so you have 2 rectangles. Wrap one around the bottom of the cake; it should reach halfway around. Wrap the other rectangle around the remaining bottom of the cake, trimming any excess. Make sure the edges of the dark green and light green fondant meet. Use a toothpick to score vertical lines in the light green fondant to make Nessie's belly scales.

3. Carefully lift the tier and slide it over the cake armature pipe to rest on the cake board.

4. Repeat steps 1 through 3 for the 8-inch (20-cm) cake tier.

5. Cover the entire 4-inch (10-cm) cake layer with dark green fondant. Cut a hole in the top of the fondant. Slide the layer over the pipe to rest on the other two tiers.

6. Roll out the blue fondant to about ⅛ inch (3 mm) thick and cut out different size circles for Nessie's spots. Attach them all over the dark green fondant of Nessie's body with a small dab of water each. Use an empty icing tip to press circular indents into Nessie's body for scales.

Add Support for Nessie's Head

1. Take the remaining 4-inch (10-cm) cake board and trim two of the sides to make an elongated rectangle with rounded corners. With a toothpick, lightly score a line dividing the rectangle in half lengthwise. Cut a ¾-inch (2-cm) hole into the board about two-thirds of the way along that line. Set aside.

2. Attach the pipe bushing (the T-shaped bracket) to the top of the PVC pipe with the flat side up. Using the end of a heavy spatula or small kitchen hammer, slowly tap on the sides of the bushing to move it down the pipe (don't push too hard or fast, or it will slip down into your cake). Stop when it's 6 inches (15 cm) from the top of the cake.

Make the Back of Nessie's Head and Her Tam-O'-Shanter Hat

1. In a large nonstick pot over medium-low, melt the butter.

2. Add the marshmallows and immediately take the pot off the heat. Stir continuously until the marshmallows melt. Stir in the rice cereal and mix until coated. Pour the mixture onto a piece of parchment or foil on a flat surface and allow to cool.

3. When cool enough to handle, but not yet cold or too hard, scoop half the mixture and form it into a sphere about 3 inches (7.5 cm) in diameter. Cut the ball in half. Set one half aside; this will be the top half of Nessie's head.

4. Cut the other half in half again. Take the two pieces and press them around the bottom of the PVC bracket to form the bottom half of Nessie's head.

5. Slide the cake board rectangle down the pipe onto the bracket so the long end points forward; this will support Nessie's protruding snout. Slide the top half of Nessie's head down the pipe. Use some of the extra crispy rice cereal mixture to "glue" the top and bottom of the head together around the back of the cake board.

6. Use the remaining crispy cereal mixture to form a flat, round hat 4 inches (10 cm) in diameter and 1 inch (2.5 cm) thick. Set aside.

Make Nessie's Neck and the Rest of Her Head

1. Knead the white modeling chocolate until soft. Roll two 1-inch (2.5-cm) balls for Nessie's eyes. Roll out the modeling chocolate and cut out 6 triangles for Nessie's teeth. Dye a walnut-size piece of white modeling chocolate red. Wrap all pieces in plastic wrap and set aside.

2. Divide the rest of the white modeling chocolate into four equal pieces. Use green food coloring to dye one piece dark green and set aside. Recombine the remaining pieces into one larger piece and use green food coloring to dye it light green.

3. Press the green modeling chocolate around the PVC pipe as you would with modeling clay from the bottom of Nessie's chin to the top of the cake to make her neck, using the photo as a reference.

4. Use green modeling chocolate to form a snout on top of the cake board support. Wrap Nessie's entire head and snout in green modeling chocolate. Add small round green freckles along the sides of her snout. Use a flat knife or modeling tool to carve out Nessie's nostrils.

5. Attach the white eyeballs to the head with toothpicks. Use green modeling chocolate to make upper and lower eyelids, using the photo as a reference.

6. Attach the teeth to Nessie's mouth using dabs of water.

Make Nessie's Tail and Flippers

1. Bend the cake wire into a 10-inch (25-cm) tail with a three-pronged tip. Wrap with foil to bulk the tail up, leaving the bottom 2 inches (5 cm) uncovered. Cover the tip with dark green modeling chocolate and the rest of the tail with green modeling chocolate. Set aside.

2. Use dark green modeling chocolate to make two 5-inch (12-cm) long flippers and two 4-inch (10-cm) long flippers. Attach a layer of green chocolate for shading, using the photo as a reference. Use a toothpick or sharp knife to carve details. Attach the two bigger flippers to the bottom cake tier and the two smaller flippers to the second cake tier using cake wire.

3. Use dark green modeling chocolate to cut out Nessie's ears. Attach a layer of green chocolate for shading, using a toothpick or knife to score details. Attach to the sides of Nessie's head using cake wire.

4. Roll out 2 strips of light green fondant and attach to the front of Nessie's neck and tail. Score on scales.

5. Press Nessie's tail into the back of the cake.

Finish Nessie's Hat

1. Knead the brown modeling chocolate until soft and wrap the crispy cereal hat in it. Press onto the top of the PVC pipe. Roll one 1½-inch (4-cm) ball out of brown modeling chocolate and attach it to the top of the hat with a toothpick. Use a sharp knife or a crumpled ball of foil to add texture.

2. Use red and black food coloring and a paintbrush to paint a plaid pattern on the hat and shade the ball. Paint black slits on Nessie's eyeballs.

3. Unwrap the red modeling chocolate. Form it into a ribbon and attach it to the bottom of the hat just over Nessie's eye using cake wire.

3, 2, 1 . . . Ya' done!

JACQUES' CHOCOLATE ADVENTURE CAKE

Season 6, Episode 3, "C'est Jacques!"

Makes one 6-layer, rainbow-topped mountain cake

We've saved the biggest and best for last: a cake featuring Mr. Chocolate himself, Jacques Torres, on a cacao-harvesting adventure into nature! This spicy chocolate cake is covered in modeling chocolate flowers and foliage, features a chocolate river, and is filled with two kinds of chocolate buttercream. For the buttercream, use the highest-quality chocolate you can find; we're partial to Jacques Torres Chocolate, naturally.

FOR THE CAKE

8 cups (1 kg) all-purpose flour

2 cups (190 g) unsweetened cocoa

8 teaspoons baking powder

4 teaspoons baking soda

½ teaspoon salt

16 large eggs

8 cups (1.6 kg) sugar

2⅔ cups (500 g) unsalted butter

4 teaspoons vanilla extract

4 cups (960 ml) whole milk

2 teaspoons cayenne pepper

FOR THE BUTTERCREAM

2 cups (4 sticks/450 g) unsalted butter, room temperature, cut into chunks

8 cups (1 kg) powdered sugar

4 teaspoons vanilla extract

¼ teaspoon salt

¼ cup (60 ml) whole milk

6 ounces (170 g) white chocolate, melted

6 ounces (170 g) dark chocolate, melted

½ cup (50 g) unsweetened cocoa

FOR THE RICE CEREAL CLOUDS

3 tablespoons unsalted butter

2¼ cups (113 g) mini marshmallows

3 cups (45 g) crispy rice cereal

FOR THE DECORATIONS

8 ounces (225 g) white fondant

6 pounds (2.7 kg) white modeling chocolate

24 ounces (680 g) brown modeling chocolate

Red, orange, yellow, green, blue, purple, gray, and skin-colored food coloring

Cornstarch

(continued on page 128)

SPECIAL EQUIPMENT

9 by 13-inch (23 by 33-cm) baking pan

Two 8-inch (20-cm) round cake pans

Three 6-inch (15-cm) round cake pans

One 8-inch (20-cm) round cake board

One 6-inch (15-cm) round cake board

¾-inch (2-cm) diameter PVC pipe rated for drinking water, 12 inches (30.5 cm) long

One ¾ by ½-inch (20 by 12-mm) PVC slip-reducing bushing

Spade drill bit, ¾ inch (2 cm) diameter

13 by 17-inch (33 by 43-cm) MDF wooden board

Foil or food-safe paper

Hot glue gun and glue

One 9-inch (23-cm) piece of 18-gauge food-safe floral or cake wire

Toothpicks

Food-safe paintbrush

Build the Cake Armature

1. To keep jungle Jacques and this rainbow-topped, chocolate adventure from crashing over, we'll need to build some quick cake armature out of PVC pipe. Make sure to get PVC pipe that's rated for drinking water, as it's considered food safe and doesn't need to be wrapped in foil (give it a good scrub before using it though!).

2. Cut off the smaller end of PVC bushing so that it will slide completely onto the PVC pipe. (You can cut it with a PVC cutter, or a hacksaw, or ask an employee at the hardware store where you buy it to cut it for you.) Set aside. When we push the bushing onto the pipe later, it should be an extremely snug fit.

3. Draw a line lengthwise down the center of the MDF board. About three-quarters of the way down that line, drill a ¾-inch (2-cm) hole into, but not all the way through, the board. Cover the cake base with foil or food-safe paper, leaving the hole open, to make the cake base. Line the inside of the hole with hot glue. Insert the PVC pipe. Allow to set.

4. Cut a ¾-inch (2-cm) hole through the center of the cake boards. Set aside.

Make the Cake

1. Since most kitchen mixers can't accommodate the batter for a cake this large, we're going to quarter the recipe and make it four times.

2. Preheat the oven to 350°F (175°C). Grease all of the baking pans. Cut out pieces of parchment paper for each pan and place in the bottoms.

3. In a large bowl, sift together 2 cups (250 g) of the flour, ½ cup (50 g) of the cocoa, 2 teaspoons of the baking powder, 1 teaspoon of the baking soda, and ⅛ teaspoon of the salt.

4. In another large bowl, using an electric mixer, combine 4 of the eggs, 2 cups (400 g) of the sugar, ⅔ cup (150 g) of the butter, 1 teaspoon of the vanilla, 1 cup (240 ml) of the milk, and ½ teaspoon of the cayenne. Add the dry mixture a large spoonful at a time and mix until just combined. Do not overmix. Use a spatula to scrape the sides and bottom of the bowl to incorporate the last bits of dry ingredients.

5. Divide the batter among the pans, filling halfway. Repeat steps 1 through 4 three more times to make a total of one 9 by 13-inch (23 by 33-cm) cake, two 8-inch (20-cm) cakes, and three 6-inch (15-cm) cakes.

6. Bake for 24 to 28 minutes, until a toothpick inserted in the center comes out clean. Let cool.

Make the Buttercream

1. We need a *lot* of buttercream for this recipe, and most mixers can't handle this much powdered sugar at one time, so we'll make it in two batches.

2. In a large bowl, using an electric mixer, beat 1 cup (2 sticks/225 g) of the butter until creamy, about 1 minute.

3. Add 4 cups (500 g) of the powdered sugar 1 cup (125 g) at a time, mixing until well combined.

4. Add 2 teaspoons of the vanilla, ⅛ teaspoon of the salt, and 2 tablespoons (30 ml) of the milk, and mix on high until thick and creamy. If the buttercream is too thin, add more powdered sugar, 1 tablespoon at a time. If the buttercream is too thick, add more milk, 1 tablespoon at a time.

5. Repeat with the remaining buttercream ingredients to make a second batch.

6. Gently stir the melted white chocolate into one batch. Gently stir the melted dark chocolate and cocoa into the other batch.

Make the Crispy Rice Cereal Clouds

1. In a large nonstick pot over medium-low, melt the butter.

2. Add the marshmallows and immediately take the pot off the heat. Stir continuously until the marshmallows melt. Stir in the rice cereal and mix until coated. Pour the mixture onto a piece of parchment or foil on a flat surface and allow to cool.

3. When cool enough to handle, but not yet cold or too hard, scoop up the mixture and form it into a cloud bank about 4 inches (10 cm) wide.

4. Lightly dust a flat surface with cornstarch. Roll out the white fondant to about ¼ inch (6 mm) thick. Wrap it around the rice cereal clouds, smoothing with your fingers. Set aside.

Stack the Cakes

1. Remove the 9 by 13-inch (23 by 33-cm) cake from its pan and remove the parchment paper. Cut the cake in half crosswise. Cut a ¾-inch (2-cm) hole in the center of one half. Carefully slide the cake over the PVC pipe armature to rest on the cake base. Set the other half of the cake in front of it on the cake base. Cover the entire layer in chocolate buttercream.

2. Run a butter knife around the edge of one of the 8-inch (20-cm) cake pans. Place a plate over the pan and flip. Tap the bottom until the cake slips out. Remove the parchment paper. If the cake has a domed top, flip it over and cut it off with a large, serrated knife so the top is level. Set the cake on the 8-inch (20-cm) cake board. Cut out a ¾-inch (2-cm) hole in the center. With a spatula (an offset spatula works great if you have one), spread a layer of white buttercream over the top. Repeat with the second 8-inch (20-cm) cake, then set it on top of the other cake. Set aside.

3. Run a butter knife around the edge of one of the 6-inch (15-cm) cake pans. Place a plate over the pan and flip. Tap the bottom until the cake slips out. Remove the parchment paper. If the cake has a domed top, flip it over and cut it off with a large, serrated knife so the top is level. Set it on the 6-inch (15-cm) cake board. Cut out a ¾-inch (2-cm) hole in the center. Spread a layer of white buttercream over the top. Repeat with the other two 6-inch (15-cm) cakes, setting the cakes atop one another.

4. Carefully stack the 6-inch (15-cm) tier on top of the 8-inch (20-cm) tier. Using a serrated knife, carve the cake into a mountain shape. Remove the 6-inch (15-cm) tier. Carefully slide the 8-inch tier over the PVC pipe onto the rectangular bottom cake. Slide the 6-inch (15-cm) tier over the PVC pipe to rest on the 8-inch (20-cm) tier. Cover both tiers in chocolate buttercream. Cover the remaining exposed PVC pipe in chocolate buttercream.

5. Carve a ¾-inch (2-cm) hole 1 inch (2.5 cm) deep into the bottom of the fondant-covered clouds. Secure onto the top of the PVC pipe.

Make the Chocolate Ropes

1. Knead the brown modeling chocolate until soft. Roll one rope, about ¼ inch (6 mm) thick and 7 inches (17 cm) long, for Jacques to hold. Set aside.

2. Roll a dozen thicker ropes, about ½ inch (12 mm) thick and 7 to 12 inches (43 to 30.5 cm) long. Attach down the top of the buttercream-covered PVC pipe as if they were raining down from the clouds. Make more ropes to trail down the side of the mountain like a chocolate waterfall.

Make the Chocolate Jungle

1. Knead the white modeling chocolate until soft. Color 8 ounces (225 g) of it gray. Roll it into 20 boulders of different sizes. Attach them all around the cake and at the bottom of the chocolate waterfall.

2. Color 2 pounds (910 g) of the white modeling chocolate green. Roll one rope about ¼ inch (6 mm) thick and 6 inches (15 cm) long and set it aside for the rainbow. Roll out the rest into a flat sheet. Tear off pieces and press them into the cake for greenery. Cut out enough palm leaves to cover front and sides of the bottom rectangular cake, then attach them to the cake.

3. Color a pinch of white modeling chocolate blue. Roll one rope about ¼ inch (6 mm) thick and 6 inches (15 cm) long and set it aside for the rainbow. Repeat for a purple rope.

4. Color 16 ounces (455 g) of the white modeling chocolate red. Roll one rope about ¼ inch (6 mm) thick and 6 inches (15 cm) long and set it aside for the rainbow. Make 10 small and 10 medium flower shapes. Attach them all over the mountain. Make 25 cacao pod shapes. Attach them all over the green leaves on the bottom of the cake.

5. Color 16 ounces (455 g) of the white modeling chocolate orange. Roll one rope about ¼ inch (6 mm) thick and 6 inches (15 cm) long and set it aside for the rainbow. Make 10 small and 10 medium flowers. Attach them all over the mountain. Make 25 cacao pod shapes. Attach them all over the green jungle leaves on the bottom of the cake.

6. Color 12 ounces (340 g) of the white modeling chocolate yellow. Roll one rope about ¼ inch (6 mm) thick and 6 inches (15 cm) long and set it aside for the rainbow. Make 25 cacao pod shapes. Attach them all over the green jungle leaves on the bottom of the cake.

7. Combine golf ball–sized chunks of white and brown modeling chocolate to make a light brown. Roll 8 thick ropes about ½ inch (12 mm) thick and add to the center of the waterfall.

8. Fill a piping bag with white buttercream and pipe the waterfall and spray around the rocks, using the photo as a reference.

Make Jacques

1. Color a golf ball–size chunk of white modeling chocolate skin-colored. Lighten a walnut-size chunk of green modeling chocolate by mixing it with some white to make light green.

2. Shape floral wire into a skeleton of Jacques climbing. Crumple foil to make the head and bulk up his body.

3. Use light green modeling chocolate to make Jacques' shirt by pressing it directly onto the foil and shaping it as necessary. Use brown modeling chocolate to make his shorts.

4. Use skin-colored chocolate to make Jacques' head, arms, and legs. Use brown modeling chocolate to make his hat and boots. Use white modeling chocolate to add socks and eyes. Use brown modeling chocolate to add pupils to his eyes. Use red modeling chocolate to add a safety harness around his waist.

5. Use a toothpick to etch details into Jacques. Use toothpicks to secure Jacques' feet into the side of the mountain. Place the 7-inch (17-cm) chocolate rope in his hand and wrap it around his waist. Attach the top of the rope to the top of the mountain.

The Rainbow Finish

1. Bend the 9-inch (23-cm) piece of cake wire into a rainbow curve.

2. Line the rainbow ropes up in order: red on top, followed by orange, yellow, green, blue, and purple. Gently press together and press into the rainbow-shaped wire. Trim 1 inch (2.5 cm) off each end so that the wire is exposed. Carefully press the ends of the wire into the top of the clouds.

3, 2, 1 . . . Ya' done!

'Tis the season for
BAKING AND EATING
ALL THE THINGS.
THESE
WINTER-THEMED
RECIPES ARE
FULL OF HOLIDAY
CHEER, HORRIBLE
CHALLENGES, AND
FA-LA-LA-LA-FUN!

Nailed It!

**NAILED IT!
HOLIDAY!**

JACQUES' LEGENDARY HOT CHOCOLATE

Nailed It! Holiday! Season 1, Episode 4, "It's a Family A-fail"

Makes 4 cups (960 ml) hot chocolate

While the contestants made hot cocoa (hot milk mixed with sweetened cocoa powder), we're going to take it up a notch by making hot chocolate: hot milk mixed with, you guessed it, melted chocolate, using Jacques' famous recipe.

3 cups (720 ml) whole milk

6 ounces (170 g) Jacques Torres 60% dark chocolate discs

½ cup (65 g) dry milk powder

1 teaspoon cornstarch

Whipped cream or marshmallows, for topping

Make the Hot Chocolate

1. In a medium pot over medium-high, bring the milk to a boil. Reduce the heat to medium.

2. Add the chocolate, whisking vigorously until it is completely melted.

3. Add the milk powder and cornstarch. Continue to whisk until everything is dissolved and the mixture is smooth and thick.

4. Divide the hot chocolate among four mugs. Top with a large dollop of whipped cream or marshmallows.

Variation #1: Frozen Hot Chocolate

1. Complete steps 1 through 3 on the left.

2. Pour the hot chocolate into a glass bowl and refrigerate overnight. The next day, the mixture will be thick, like pudding.

3. Blend the mixture with ice, then divide among four glasses. Top with whipped cream or marshmallows.

Variation #2: Frappé

1. Complete steps 1 through 3 on the left.

2. Pour the hot chocolate into cocktail shaker filled with ice. Shake and strain into four glasses.

3, 2, 1 . . . Ya' done!

PANIC **CAN'T FIND JACQUES TORRES CHOCOLATE**

It's available online at mrchocolate.com, or you can substitute your favorite brand.

WINTRY CABIN

Nailed It! Holiday! Season 1, Episode 4, "It's a Family A-fail"

Makes 1 cabin

This cozy mini cabin is made entirely of crispy rice cereal treat and can be customized with whatever colors or decorations you desire.

FOR THE CRISPY RICE CEREAL TREAT

7 tablespoons (96 g) unsalted butter

5¼ cups (263 g) mini marshmallows

12 ounces (340 g) semisweet chocolate chips

7 cups (105 g) crispy rice cereal

FOR THE BUTTERCREAM

1 cup (2 sticks/225 g) unsalted butter, softened

4 cups (500 g) powdered sugar

2 teaspoons vanilla extract

⅛ teaspoon salt

¼ cup (60 ml) whole milk

FOR THE DECORATIONS

Red, green, and brown food coloring

Shaved white coconut or white sprinkles

12 ounces (340 g) white fondant

Cornstarch

Edible gold paint

Food-safe paintbrush

Make the Cabin Walls

1. In a large nonstick pot over medium-low, melt 5 tablespoons (68 g) of the butter.

2. Add 3¾ cups (188 g) marshmallows and immediately take the pot off the heat. Stir continuously until the marshmallows melt. Add the chocolate and stir until melted.

3. Add 5 cups (75 g) of the rice cereal and mix until coated. Pour the mixture onto a piece of parchment or foil on a flat surface and allow to cool.

4. When cool enough to handle, but not yet cold or too hard, split the mixture in half. Use one half to build a solid rectangle and solid triangular prism for the cabin and attic. Set the triangular shape on top of the rectangle.

5. Use the other half of the mixture to roll out chocolate "logs" and cut to fit the sides of the cabin. Set aside.

Make the Cabin Roof

1. In a medium nonstick pot over medium-low, melt the remaining 2 tablespoons butter.

2. Add the remaining marshmallows and immediately take the pot off the heat. Add a few drops of green food coloring. Stir continuously until the marshmallows melt and the cream is green.

3. Stir in 2 cups (30 g) rice cereal and mix until coated. Pour the mixture onto a piece of parchment or foil on a flat surface and allow to cool.

4. When cool enough to handle, but not yet cold or too hard, form two flat rectangles a little longer and wider than the cabin pieces for the roof pieces. Set aside.

Make the Buttercream

1. In a large bowl, using an electric mixer, beat the butter until creamy, about 1 minute.

2. Add the powdered sugar 1 cup (125 g) at a time, mixing until well combined.

3. Add the vanilla, salt, and milk, and mix on high until thick and creamy. If the buttercream is too thin, add more powdered sugar, 1 tablespoon at a time. If the buttercream is too thick, add more milk, 1 tablespoon at a time.

Assemble the Cabin

1. Use buttercream to stick the roof pieces onto the cabin.

2. Use buttercream to attach the logs to the walls of the cabin, leaving some buttercream visible between the logs.

3. Spread buttercream around the edge of the roof.

Decorate!

1. Sprinkle coconut or white sprinkles on the buttercream at the roof edges.

2. Pull off a pinch of white fondant and set aside. Divide the rest of the fondant into three pieces. Dye one brown, one green, and one red.

3. Lightly dust a flat surface with cornstarch. Roll out the red fondant and cut out a door. Attach it to the front of the cabin using buttercream.

4. Roll out the brown fondant and cut out wooden beams to frame the door. Add wood grain details with a toothpick or sharp knife. Attach around the door using buttercream.

5. Roll out the green fondant and cut out green leaves for the wreath. Attach it to the door with buttercream.

6. Form the white fondant into a tiny bow for the wreath. Paint it gold.

3, 2, 1 . . . Ya' done!

SKI VACATION FLANNEL CAKE

Nailed It! Holiday! Season 1, Episode 2, "Winter Blunderland"

Makes one 3-tier, 8-layer mountain cake

Chocolate penguin skiers take to the slopes on this Door #2 challenge of a mountain resort cake. Covered in snowy buttercream, this eight-layer cake is made of rich chocolate and red velvet cake layered in a checkerboard style that evokes a cozy lumberjack plaid and stuffed with chocolate buttercream. And to give you slightly more of a break than we give our contestants, we're going to make a simpler version of the plaid cake pattern using cake rings instead of strips.

FOR THE CHOCOLATE CAKE

4 cups (500 g) flour

1 cup (95 g) unsweetened cocoa

4 teaspoons baking powder

2 teaspoons baking soda

¼ teaspoon salt

8 large eggs

4 cups (800 g) sugar

1⅓ cups (300 g) unsalted butter, melted

2 teaspoons vanilla extract

2 cups (480 ml) whole milk

FOR THE RED VELVET CAKE

5⅓ cups (665 g) all-purpose flour

6 tablespoons (38 g) unsweetened cocoa

2 teaspoons salt

4 cups (800 g) sugar

2½ cups (600 ml) vegetable oil

8 large eggs

4 teaspoons red food coloring

2 cups (480 ml) buttermilk

4 teaspoons baking soda

¼ cup (60 ml) white vinegar

FOR THE CHOCOLATE BUTTERCREAM

1½ cups (3 sticks/340 g) unsalted butter, room temperature, cut into chunks

⅔ cup (65 g) unsweetened cocoa

2 teaspoons vanilla extract

¼ teaspoon salt

⅔ cup (115 g) semisweet chocolate chips, melted

8 cups (1 kg) powdered sugar

¼ cup (60 ml) whole milk

FOR THE WHITE BUTTERCREAM

2 cups (4 sticks/450 g) unsalted butter, room temperature, cut into chunks

8 cups (1 kg) powdered sugar

4 teaspoons vanilla extract

¼ teaspoon salt

¼ cup (60 ml) whole milk

(continued on page 141)

FOR THE DECORATIONS

Edible glitter, clear or white

16 ounces (455 g) brown modeling chocolate

16 ounces (455 g) white modeling chocolate

16 ounces (455 g) black modeling chocolate

16 ounces (455 g) green fondant

Red, yellow, and blue food coloring

Cornstarch

SPECIAL EQUIPMENT

Two 10-inch (25-cm) round cake pans

Two 8-inch (20-cm) round cake pans

Two 6-inch (15-cm) round cake pans

Cake base or three 14-inch (35.5-cm) cake boards taped together and wrapped in foil

One 8-inch (20-cm) round cake board

One 6-inch (15-cm) round cake board

Nine cake dowel rods

Food-safe paintbrush

Toothpicks

Make the Chocolate Cakes

1. Since most kitchen mixers can't accommodate the batter for this many cakes at once, we're going to split the job in half.

2. Preheat the oven to 350°F (175°C). Grease two 10-inch (25-cm), one 8-inch (20-cm), and one 6-inch (15-cm) round cake pans. Cut out a circle of parchment paper for each pan and place in the bottoms.

3. In a large bowl, sift together 2 cups (250 g) of the flour, ½ cup (50 g) of the cocoa, 2 teaspoons of the baking powder, 1 teaspoon of the baking soda, and ⅛ teaspoon of the salt.

4. In another large bowl, using an electric mixer, combine 4 of the eggs, 2 cups (400 g) of the sugar, ⅔ cup (150 g) of the butter, 1 teaspoon of the vanilla, and 1 cup (240 ml) of the milk. Add the dry mixture a large spoonful at a time and mix until just combined. Do not overmix. Use a spatula to scrape the sides and bottom of the bowl to incorporate the last bits of dry ingredients.

5. Divide the batter between one 10-inch (25-cm) and one 8-inch (20-cm) pan, filling halfway, and bake for 24 to 28 minutes, until a toothpick inserted in the center comes out clean. Let cool.

6. Repeat with the remaining cake ingredients, dividing the batter between one 10-inch (25-cm) and one 6-inch (15-cm) pan, filling halfway, and bake for 24 to 28 minutes, until a toothpick inserted in the center comes out clean. Let cool.

7. Remove all the chocolate cakes from their pans and remove the parchment paper. Wash and dry the 10-inch (25-cm) pans so you can use them again for the red velvet cakes.

Make the Red Velvet Cakes

1. Since most kitchen mixers can't accommodate the batter for this many cakes at once, we're going to split the job in half.

2. Preheat the oven to 350°F (175°C). Grease two 10-inch (25-cm), one 8-inch (20-cm), and one 6-inch (15-cm) round cake pans. Cut out a circle of parchment paper for each pan and place in the bottoms.

3. In a medium bowl, sift together 2⅔ cups (330 g) of the flour, 3 tablespoons of the cocoa, and 1 teaspoon of the salt.

4. In a large bowl, using an electric mixer on medium speed, beat 2 cups (400 g) of the sugar and 1¼ cups (300 ml) of the oil until combined. Add 4 of the eggs and 2 teaspoons of the red food coloring, scraping down sides to incorporate fully. Reduce the speed to low. Add the flour mixture and 1 cup (240 ml) of the buttermilk, alternating, until fully mixed.

5. In a small bowl, combine 2 teaspoons of the baking soda and 2 tablespoons of the vinegar (it will bubble and foam!). Add this to the batter and mix to combine.

6. Divide the batter between one 10-inch (25-cm) and one 8-inch (20-cm) pan, filling halfway, and bake for 20 to 23 minutes, until a toothpick inserted in the center comes out clean. Let cool.

7. Repeat with the remaining cake ingredients, dividing the batter between one 10-inch (25-cm) and one 6-inch (15-cm) pan, filling halfway, and bake for 20 to 23 minutes, until a toothpick inserted in the center comes out clean. Let cool.

8. Remove all the red velvet cakes from their pans and remove the parchment paper.

Make the Chocolate Buttercream

1. We need a *lot* of buttercream for this recipe, and most mixers can't handle this much powdered sugar at one time, so we'll make it in two batches.

2. In a large bowl, using an electric mixer, beat ¾ cup (1½ sticks/170 g) of the butter until creamy, about 1 minute.

3. Add ⅓ cup (30 g) of the cocoa, 1 teaspoon of the vanilla, and ⅛ teaspoon of the salt and beat until smooth. Beat in ⅓ cup (75 ml) of the melted semisweet chocolate.

4. Add 4 cups (500 g) of the powdered sugar 1 cup (125 g) at a time, mixing until well combined.

5. Add 2 tablespoons (30 ml) of the milk and mix on high until thick and creamy. If the buttercream is too thin, add more powdered sugar, 1 tablespoon at a time. If the buttercream is too thick, add more milk, 1 tablespoon at a time.

6. Repeat with the remaining chocolate buttercream ingredients to make a second batch.

PANIC

FROSTING AVALANCHE

Ski mountains require a lot of frosting. If you're not keen to make this much yourself, you can save time by buying it premade. You'll need 8 cans of white whipped frosting, based on a typical can size of 12 to 14 oz (340 to 397 g).

Give the Cakes a "Plaid" Pattern

1. If any of the cakes has a domed top, flip it over and cut it off with a large, serrated knife so the top is level.

2. Trace the bottom of the 10-inch (25-cm) pan onto a piece of parchment paper. Using other round items in your kitchen, like bowls or glasses, or a compass, trace three more concentric circles inside the larger circle.

3. Cut out the circles so you have a center circle and 3 rings made of parchment. Line the parchment templates up on the surface of one of the 10-inch (25-cm) cakes, securing them with toothpicks, and cut along the lines with a sharp knife. Repeat with the other three 10-inch (25-cm) cakes.

4. Remove the outer circle of each cake and set aside. You should have 2 chocolate rings and 2 red velvet rings. Remove the next circle from the cakes and place them inside the outer circles, alternating colors, so a chocolate outer ring will have a red velvet ring next, and vice versa. Continue this process with the other rings, rebuilding the cakes with alternating color rings.

5. Place a dab of chocolate buttercream on the center of the cake base. Carefully transfer one of the colored ring layers onto the board. With a spatula (an offset spatula works great if you have one), spread a layer of chocolate buttercream on top, then repeat with the remaining layers, alternating the outer color, until you have a four-layer tier.

6. Discard the largest parchment circle and use the smaller ones to repeat steps 1 through 5 with the 8-inch (20-cm) cakes.

7. Place a dab of chocolate buttercream on the center of the 8-inch (20-cm) cake board. Carefully place one of the colored ring layers onto the board. Spread a layer of chocolate buttercream on top, then repeat with the remaining layer. Set aside.

8. Discard the next largest parchment circle and use the smaller ones to repeat steps 1 through 5 with the 6-inch (15-cm) cakes.

9. Place a dab of chocolate buttercream on the center of the 6-inch (15-cm) cake board. Carefully place one of the colored ring layers onto the board. Spread a layer of chocolate buttercream on top, then repeat with the remaining layer. Set aside.

Stack the Cakes

1. Hold a dowel next to the bottom 10-inch (25-cm) tier and mark the height on the dowel. Cut five dowels to that length. Press one dowel into the center of the cake and press four more around it, spacing them out for support, but staying at least 2 inches (5 cm) from the edge.

2. Set the 8-inch (20-cm) cake tier on top of the bottom tier. Hold a dowel next to the tier and mark the height on the dowel. Cut four dowels to that length. Press the dowels into the cake, spacing them out for support, but staying at least 2 inches (5 cm) from the edge.

3. Set the 6-inch (15-cm) cake tier on top.

4. Using a large, serrated knife, carve the cake into a dome or mountain shape, starting at the top and sloping downward.

Make the White Buttercream

1. Again, we need a *lot* of buttercream, so we'll make it in two batches.

2. Using a mixer, beat 1 cup (2 sticks/225 g) of the butter until creamy, about 1 minute.

3. Add 4 cups (500 g) of the powdered sugar 1 cup (125 g) at a time, mixing until well combined.

4. Add 2 teaspoons of the vanilla, ⅛ teaspoon of the salt, and 2 tablespoons (30 ml) of the milk, and mix on high until thick and creamy. If the buttercream is too thin, add more powdered sugar, 1 tablespoon at a time. If the buttercream is too thick, add more milk, 1 tablespoon at a time.

5. Repeat with the remaining buttercream ingredients to make a second batch.

6. Cover the entire cake mountain in white buttercream, including the cake base, making swirls for the snow.

Decorate!

1. Sprinkle edible glitter all over the mountain while the buttercream is still wet so it sticks.

2. Knead the brown modeling chocolate until soft. Make 20 boulders of various sizes. Stick them all over the cake, including making a cliff edge, using the photo on page 138 as a reference.

3. Make five T shapes connected by thin ropes for the ski lift and place on the cake base and slightly up the side. Make a thin flagpole about 1 to 2 inches (2.5 to 5 cm) tall.

4. Knead the white modeling chocolate until soft. Cut a small rolled-out piece of it to make a flag. Attach it to the flagpole using a dab of water. Use a paintbrush to spell out a message on the flag. Set aside to let dry.

5. Take a golf ball–size chunk of white modeling chocolate and color it yellow. Color another chunk blue, and one red.

6. Use black and white modeling chocolate to make penguins (the original cake has 13 penguins). Use yellow modeling chocolate to add beaks and feet. Use blue and red modeling chocolate to add skis, snowboards, hats, and goggles. Secure to the cake with toothpicks.

7. Lightly dust a flat surface with cornstarch. Roll out the green fondant. Cut out shapes to make 20 trees (tip: scissors work really well for making pines)—you can either make 2D tree shapes or, if you feel up for a challenge, cut out many small triangles and form them together into cone-shaped 3D trees. Secure to the cake with toothpicks. You can dab extra white buttercream on top of the trees to look like snow.

8. Add the flag to the very top using a toothpick. Cover the entire scene in more glitter.

3, 2, 1 . . . Ya' done!

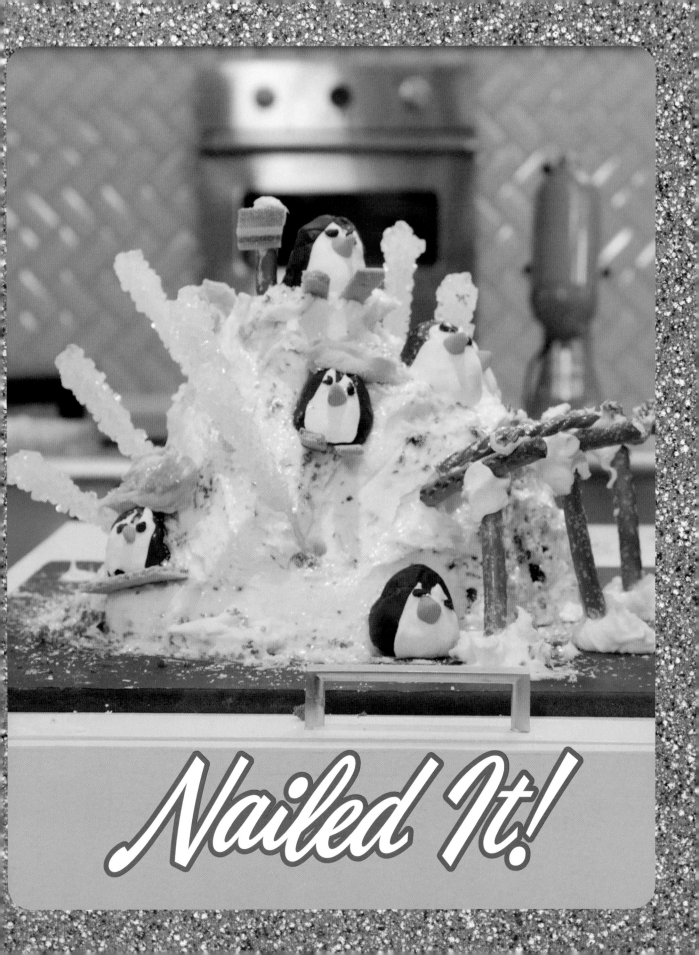

SYLVIA WEINSTOCK HANUKKAH CAKE

Nailed It! Holiday! Season 1, Episode 4, "You Mitzvah Spot!"

Makes one 3-tier, 9-layer cake

Sylvia Weinstock created this special Hanukkah-themed cake just for us, with nine purple layers flavored with kosher wine, nine fondant candles lit with poured sugar flames, and, of course, her signature glasses.

FOR THE CAKE

7½ cups (875 g) all-purpose flour

2 tablespoons baking powder

1 tablespoon baking soda

¾ teaspoon kosher salt

12 large eggs

6 cups (1.2 kg) sugar

3 cups (6 sticks/675 g) unsalted butter, melted

2 tablespoons purple food coloring

3 cups (720 ml) red kosher wine

FOR THE BUTTERCREAM

2½ cups (5 sticks/265 g) unsalted butter, softened

10 cups (1.2 kg) powdered sugar

5 teaspoons vanilla extract

½ teaspoon salt

⅔ cup (165 ml) whole milk

FOR THE DECORATIONS

24 ounces (680 ml) white fondant

16 ounces (455 g) dark blue fondant

4 ounces (115 g) black fondant

Dark blue and turquoise food coloring

Edible gold paint

4 ounces (115 g) yellow isomalt sticks

2 ounces (55 g) red isomalt sticks

2 ounces (55 g) orange isomalt sticks

Cornstarch

SPECIAL EQUIPMENT

Three 10-inch (25-cm) square cake pans

Three 8-inch (20-cm) square cake pans

Three 6-inch (15-cm) square cake pans

Cake base or three 14-inch (35.5-cm) square cake boards taped together and wrapped in foil

One 8-inch (20-cm) square cake board

One 6-inch (15-cm) square cake board

18 cake dowel rods

Food-safe paintbrush

Toothpicks

Nonstick silicone baking mat or liner, such as a Silpat

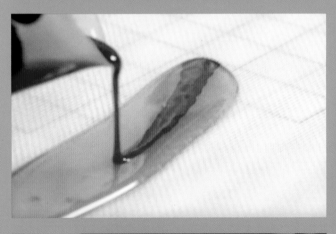

Make the Cake

1. Since most kitchen mixers can't accommodate the batter for this many cakes at once, we're going to split the job into three batches. This will also allow you to wash and reuse cake pans if you need to.

2. Preheat the oven to 350°F (175°C). Grease the cake pans. Cut out a square of parchment paper for each pan and place in the bottoms.

3. In a large bowl, sift together 2½ cups (315 g) of the flour, 2 teaspoons of the baking powder, 1 teaspoon of the baking soda, and ¼ teaspoon of the salt.

4. In another large bowl, using an electric mixer, combine 4 of the eggs, 2 cups (400 g) of the sugar, 1 cup (2 sticks/225 g) of the butter, 2 teaspoons of the purple food coloring, and 1 cup (240 ml) of the kosher wine. Add the dry mixture a large spoonful at a time and mix until just combined. Do not overmix. Use a spatula to scrape the sides and bottom of the bowl to incorporate the last bits of dry ingredients.

5. Divide the batter among the pans, filling half-way. Repeat with the remaining cake ingredients in two batches, dividing the batter among the remaining pans. Bake for 24 to 28 minutes, until a toothpick inserted in the center comes out clean. Let cool.

6. When cool, remove the cakes from their pans and remove the parchment paper. If a cake has a domed top, flip it over and cut it off with a large, serrated knife so the top is level.

Make the Buttercream

1. We need a *lot* of buttercream for this recipe, and most mixers can't handle this much powdered sugar at one time, so we'll make it in two batches.

2. In a large bowl, using an electric mixer, beat 1¼ cups (2½ sticks/130 g) of the butter until creamy, about 1 minute.

3. Add 5 cups (625 g) of the powdered sugar 1 cup (125 g) at a time, mixing until well combined.

4. Add 2½ teaspoons of the vanilla, ¼ teaspoon of the salt, and ⅓ cup (80 ml) of the milk, and mix on high until thick and creamy. If the buttercream is too thin, add more powdered sugar, 1 tablespoon at a time. If the buttercream is too thick, add more milk, 1 tablespoon at a time.

5. Repeat with the remaining buttercream ingredients to make a second batch.

6. Divide the buttercream into thirds. Color one third turquoise/light blue. Leave the remaining buttercream white.

Assemble the Cake

1. Place a dab of white buttercream on the center of the cake base.

2. Set one of the 10-inch (25-cm) cakes on the center of the cake board. With a spatula (an offset spatula works great if you have one), spread a layer of white buttercream on top. Repeat with the remaining two 10-inch (25-cm) cakes.

3. Hold a dowel next to the full bottom cake tier and mark the height on the dowel. Cut five dowels to that length. Press one dowel into the center of the cake and press four more around it, spacing them out for support, but staying at least 2 inches (5 cm) from the edge.

4. Place the 8-inch (20-cm) cake board on top of the bottom tier and lightly press down. Place a dab of white buttercream on the center of the cake board. Set an 8-inch (20-cm) cake on the cake board. Spread a layer of white buttercream on top. Repeat with the remaining two 8-inch (20-cm) cakes.

5. Hold a dowel next to the middle tier and mark the height on the dowel. Cut four dowels to that length. Press the dowels into the cake, spacing them out for support, but staying at least 2 inches (5 cm) from the edge.

6. Place the 6-inch (15-cm) cake board on top of the middle tier and lightly press down. Place a dab of white buttercream on the center of the cake board.

7. Set a 6-inch (15-cm) cake on the cake board. Spread a layer of white buttercream on top. Repeat with the final 6-inch (15-cm) cake.

8. Cover the bottom cake tier in a thin layer of light blue buttercream, making the edges as smooth as possible, ignoring any crumbs. (We call this the "crumb coat," and we'll be adding another layer over it.) Cover the middle tier with a thin layer of white buttercream in the same way. Finally, cover the top tier with a thin layer of light blue buttercream in the same way. Let the cake sit so the first layer of buttercream can harden.

Make the Fondant Decorations

1. Lightly dust a flat surface with cornstarch. Roll out the white fondant. Cut out 9 circles each about 2½ inches (6 cm) in diameter. Set aside.

2. Cut out 35 small circles, the size of coins around 1 inch (2.5 cm) across. Paint them gold and set aside to dry.

3. Roll out the black fondant and cut out frames for Sylvia's glasses, placing them around 2 of the large white fondant circles.

4. Spread another thin layer of light blue buttercream over the bottom tier, making it as smooth as possible. Spread another thin layer of white buttercream over the middle tier, and another layer of light blue buttercream on the top.

5. Roll out the dark blue fondant and cut thin strips to make vertical stripes and attach them to the middle tier. Attach Sylvia's glasses to the middle tier, over the stripes.

6. Attach 2 white fondant circles to the front and 2 to each of the sides of the bottom tier, and 1 white fondant circle to the front of the top tier. Paint stars and a menorah on the white circles, using the photo on page 146 as a reference.

Make the Hanukkah Candles

1. Roll white and dark blue fondant ropes and wind them together around 9 cake dowels, leaving 1½ inches (4 cm) of the dowels uncovered at the bottom.

2. Place the isomalt sticks in microwave-safe bowls. Microwave the isomalt in 15-second bursts, stirring after each. Carefully (because it will be hot!), pour the yellow melted isomalt into an oblong puddle on a lightly oiled silicone baking mat. Drizzle the red and orange melted isomalt over the yellow. Use a toothpick to swirl the colors. Let cool.

3. When the isomalt is cool but still very pliable, gently lift it off the mat and cut flame shapes with scissors. Twist the edges. Stick on top of candles.

Make the Bow on Top

Roll out dark blue fondant and cut out 12 strips, each 1½ by 8 inches (4 by 20 cm). Curl each strip over itself and stick its ends together, making loops. Cluster the loops on top of the topmost cake tier with the seams in the center to create an elaborate bow.

Decorate!

1. Press 8 candles into the top edges of the middle tier so they surround the top tier. Place 1 candle on the very top.

2. Arrange gold coins around the bottom of every layer. (If you have any wine left over, now is a good time for any adults in the kitchen to get to sippin' in celebration—or in mourning—of how your cake turned out!)

3, 2, 1 . . . Ya' done!

NICOLE AT THE POLE CAKE

Nailed It! Holiday! Season 2, Episode 4, "It's a Wonderfail Life"

Makes one 2-tier, 6-layer geode cake

Quite possibly our favorite cake, this two-tier geode cake features the lovely Nicole Byer in a green Santa suit at the North Pole with two decidedly evil elves as they pack up coal to stuff in stockings for all the rotten little children of the world. Inspired by contestant De'Jonnae Boyd, the cake is peppermint flavored. The geode mine is made from rock candy, and Nicole's kingdom of ice is covered in snow sugar.

FOR THE CAKE

7½ cups (875 g) all-purpose flour

2 tablespoons baking powder

1 tablespoon baking soda

1 teaspoon salt

12 large eggs

6 cups (1.2 kg) sugar

3 cups (720 ml) whole milk

2¼ cups (540 ml) vegetable oil

1 tablespoon peppermint extract

1 tablespoon green food coloring

FOR THE BUTTERCREAM

1½ cups (3 sticks/340 g) unsalted butter, softened

6 cups (1.2 kg) powdered sugar

1 tablespoon vanilla extract

¼ teaspoon salt

⅓ cup (80 ml) whole milk

FOR THE DECORATIONS

4 pounds (1.8 kg) white fondant

16 ounces (455 g) light blue fondant

6 ounces (170 g) semisweet chocolate, melted

1 cup (192 g) black rock candy

¼ cup (48 g) purple rock candy

16 ounces (455 g) white modeling chocolate

8 ounces (225 g) brown modeling chocolate

6 ounces (170 g) non-melting snow sugar

Red, yellow, green, and black food coloring

Cornstarch

Shortening

SPECIAL EQUIPMENT

Three 8-inch (20-cm) round cake pans

Three 6-inch (15-cm) round cake pans

Cake base or three 10-inch (25-cm) cake boards taped together and wrapped in foil

4 cake dowel rods

Food-safe paintbrush

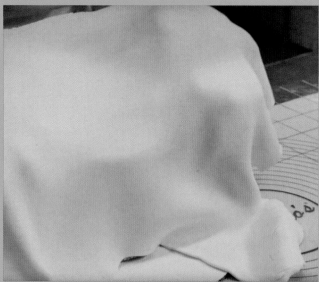

Make the Cake

1. Since most kitchen mixers can't accommodate the batter for seven cakes at once, we're going to split the job in half.

2. Preheat the oven to 350°F (175°C). Grease the cake pans. Cut out a circle of parchment paper for each pan and place in the bottoms.

3. In a large bowl, sift together 3¾ cups (438 g) of the flour, 1 tablespoon of the baking powder, 1½ teaspoons of the baking soda, and ½ teaspoon of the salt.

4. In another large bowl, using an electric mixer, combine 6 of the eggs, 3 cups (600 g) of the sugar, 1½ cups (360 ml) of the milk, 1 cup (240 ml) plus 2 tablespoons of the vegetable oil, 1½ teaspoons of the peppermint extract, and 1½ teaspoons of the green food coloring. Add the dry mixture a large spoonful at a time and mix until just combined. Do not overmix. Use a spatula to scrape the sides and bottom of the bowl to incorporate the last bits of dry ingredients.

5. Divide the batter among the pans, filling halfway. Repeat with the remaining cake ingredients, dividing the batter among the pans, filling halfway. Bake for 20 to 24 minutes, until a toothpick inserted in the center comes out clean. Let cool.

6. When cool, remove the cakes from their pans, and remove the parchment paper. If any cake layer has a domed top, flip it over and cut it off with a large, serrated knife so the top is level.

Make the Buttercream

1. We need a *lot* of buttercream for this recipe, and most mixers can't handle this much powdered sugar at one time, so we'll make it in two batches.

2. In a large bowl, using an electric mixer, beat ¾ cup (1½ sticks/170 g) of the butter until creamy, about 1 minute.

3. Add 3 cups (375 g) of the powdered sugar 1 cup (125 g) at a time, mixing until well combined.

4. Add 1½ teaspoons of the vanilla, ⅛ teaspoon of the salt, and 8 teaspoons (40 ml) of the milk, and mix on high until thick and creamy. If the buttercream is too thin, add more powdered sugar, 1 tablespoon at a time. If the buttercream is too thick, add more milk, 1 tablespoon at a time.

5. Repeat with the remaining buttercream ingredients to make a second batch.

PANIC

WHAT IS SNOW SUGAR AND WHAT IF I CAN'T FIND IT?

"Snow sugar," also called non-melting sugar topping, is a specially created sugar that won't melt in extreme heat or cold—just in your mouth. You can find it at specialty baking stores, gourmet groceries, or online. You can also substitute regular sugar crystal sprinkles.

Assemble the Cake

1. Place a dab of white buttercream on the center of the 8-inch (20-cm) cake board. Set one 8-inch (20-cm) cake on the center of the cake board. With a spatula (an offset spatula works great if you have one), spread a layer of buttercream about ¼ to ½ inch (7 to 12 mm) thick on top. Repeat for the remaining two 8-inch (20-cm) cakes. Cover the entire tier in a thin layer of buttercream; it doesn't have to be pretty since we're covering it with fondant later. Set aside.

2. Repeat with the 6-inch (15-cm) cakes. Cover the entire tier in a thin layer of buttercream. Set aside.

3. Take a large ball of white fondant and a small ball of light blue fondant and twist them together to make a marbled effect. Lightly dust a flat surface with cornstarch. Roll out the marbled fondant into a large enough circle to cover the 8-inch (20-cm) cake tier, about ⅛ inch (3 mm) thick. Drape over the cake and smooth it with your hands. Trim any excess from around the bottom. Repeat for the 6-inch (15-cm) cake tier.

4. Place a dab of buttercream on the middle of the cake base. Carefully place the fondant-covered 8-inch (20-cm) tier on the cake base. Insert 3 wooden cake dowels into the 8-inch (20-cm) cake, spacing them out for support, but staying at least 2 inches (5 cm) from the edge, leaving them exposed at the top to support the 6-inch (15-cm) layer. Carefully place the 6-inch (15-cm), fondant-covered tier on top of the 8-inch (20-cm) tier.

5. Mix a bit of the marbled fondant on the palm of your hand with a dab of shortening and press into the seams between the two tiers to blend them together.

Make the Coal Mine

1. Use a knife to cut a jagged hole in the side of the cake from the bottom up to the second tier. Remove the fondant and set aside. Use a spoon to dig out some of the cake to enlarge the hole and give it rough edges. Lay the piece of fondant back in the hole, adding extra patches as necessary so that no cake is left exposed.

2. Place the melted chocolate in a plastic baggie. Cut the corner off and pipe the chocolate into the hole. Line the hole with rock candy pieces, letting them spill out onto the cake base.

3. Outline the coal mine with gold paint.

Make the Elves

1. Knead the modeling chocolates until soft. Color a golf ball–size chunk of white modeling chocolate skin-colored. Color another chunk green, and another red. Color a smaller chunk yellow.

2. Shape floral wire into the skeleton of an elf. Add crumpled foil to make the head and bulk up his body. Repeat for a second elf.

3. Use red modeling chocolate to make the first elf's outfit by pressing it directly onto the foil and shaping it as necessary.

4. Use skin-colored chocolate to make the elf's head, arms, and legs. Use brown modeling chocolate to make his belt, boots, eyebrows, mustache, and ax. Use white modeling chocolate to add eyes. Use brown modeling chocolate to add pupils to his eyes. Use red modeling chocolate to make his hat. Use a toothpick to etch details into the elf.

5. Repeat for the second elf, using green modeling chocolate for this elf's clothing.

6. Use toothpicks to secure the elves' feet into the coal mine and bottom of the mountain.

7. Use red modeling chocolate to make 2 coal collection bags. Roll yellow modeling chocolate into a rope to wrap around the top of the bags. Fill the tops of the bags with rock candy. Place one next to the green elf, and one on the top of the cake for Nicole, securing with toothpicks.

Make Nicole

1. Mix a chunk of brown modeling chocolate with a chunk of white modeling chocolate to create Nicole's skin color. Color a chunk of white modeling chocolate light green for her clothes.

2. Shape floral wire into the skeleton of Nicole. Add crumpled foil to make the head and bulk up her body.

3. Use the light green chocolate to make Nicole's outfit by pressing it directly onto the foil and shaping it as necessary.

4. Use Nicole's skin-colored chocolate to make her head, neck, and legs. Use brown modeling chocolate to make her belt, boots, eyebrows, and pupils. Use yellow modeling chocolate to make her belt buckle.

5. Use white modeling chocolate to add a collar, hem, cuffs, gloves, and socks. Use white modeling chocolate to add eyes and teeth. Use a toothpick, sharp knife, or modeling tool to etch features into Nicole's face. DO NOT MESS UP HER BEAUTIFUL FACE! Use brown modeling chocolate to make individual curls all over Nicole's head.

Make the North Pole Sign

1. Make a thick rope out of white modeling chocolate. Make another out of red modeling chocolate. Wrap them together around a wooden dowel, leaving the bottom of the dowel free to be stuck into the cake. Add a ball of red modeling chocolate to the top of the sign.

2. Roll out the light green modeling chocolate and cut out an arrow sign. Attach it to the striped pole using a dab of water.

3. Using white paint, spell out "NORTH POLE" on the arrow. Using black paint, write "Coal" on the two red coal collection bags.

Make It Snow

Sprinkle snow sugar, or white crystal sprinkles, all over the cake.

3, 2, 1 . . . Ya' done!

NICOLE, UPON SEEING CONTESTANT DE'JONNAE'S CAKE: "THIS IS SO DISRESPECTFUL TO ME. AND I LOVE IT SO MUCH."

THE PERFECT
PARTY CHALLENGE,
THESE RECIPES ARE
DESIGNED WITH
PLENTY OF OPTIONS
so you can customize
YOUR EXPERIENCE
DEPENDING ON YOUR
SKILL SET, YOUR
COMFORT LEVEL WITH
HOT OIL, AND YOUR
PERSONAL PREFERENCE.
MIX AND MATCH EACH
OR EVERY STEP!

Nailed It!

DONUT
YOU
DARE

FLAMINGO POOL FLOAT DONUT

Nailed It! Germany, Season 1, Episode 2, "Baking in the Sun"

Makes 10 donuts

DONUT CHOICES

162
YEAST DOUGH FROM SCRATCH

PREMADE PIZZA DOUGH
After you've bought a package of pre-made pizza dough at the store, let it come to room temperature and then go straight to "Cutting the Dough"

STORE-BOUGHT DONUTS
Skip to Topping Choices!

BAKING CHOICES

163
DEEP FRIED

163
BAKED

STORE-BOUGHT DONUTS
Skip to Topping Choices!

TOPPING CHOICES

164
GLAZED

164
CANDY DIPPED

165
BUTTERCREAM FROSTED

LEVEL OF FLAMINGO DETAIL

165
BEST FLAMINGO EVER

165
BASIC BIRD SHAPE

NONE, IT MUST HAVE FLOWN AWAY

After you finish your chosen topping method from the previous list: Ya' done!

Yeast Dough from Scratch

½ cup (120 ml) warm whole milk

3 teaspoons active dry yeast

1 teaspoon plus 3 tablespoons sugar

2½ cups (270 g) all-purpose flour

4 tablespoons unsalted butter, melted

2 large eggs, room temperature

2 teaspoons vanilla extract

1. In a small glass bowl, combine the milk, yeast, and 1 teaspoon of the sugar. Cover and let sit for 10 minutes, until the mixture is foamy. If it's not, start over with fresh yeast.

2. In the bowl of a stand mixer with the dough hook, combine the flour, butter, egg, vanilla, and remaining sugar. Add the yeast mixture and knead for 2 minutes. The dough will be very wet and sticky.

3. Coat the inside of a large glass bowl with oil. Roll dough in the oil and let rise for 45 minutes or until it doubles in size.

4. Go to "Cutting the Dough" in the next column.

Cutting the Dough

1. Punch down the dough.

2. Lightly dust a flat surface with flour. Roll out the dough ½ inch (12 mm) thick. Use a 3-inch (7.5-cm) biscuit or cookie cutter (or the edge of a glass) to cut circles into the dough. Use a 1-inch (2.5-cm) circle cutter (a large icing tip will work too) to cut out holes in the center. Lay the donuts and donut holes on a floured baking sheet with space between them. Cover and let rise for 10 minutes.

3. Go to "Frying Donuts" on the next page.

Frying Donuts

Peanut, canola, or other neutral oil

SPECIAL EQUIPMENT

Oil thermometer

1. Fill your deep-fat fryer or a heavy-bottomed saucepan halfway with oil. Heat the oil to 375°F (190°C). Set a cooling rack in a baking sheet.

2. Add the donuts to the oil 2 or 3 at a time. Cook for 1 minute on each side, until golden brown. Remove the donuts to the cooling rack. Donut holes need only be fried 30 seconds on each side.

3. For glazed donuts, go to the next page.

4. For candy dipped donuts, go to the next page.

5. For buttercream frosted donuts, go to page 165.

Baked Donuts

While fried yeast donuts are lighter and crispier, these cakey rings are dense and delicious!

1 large egg

⅓ cup (80 ml) whole milk

2 tablespoons unsalted butter, melted

1 teaspoon vanilla extract

1 cup (125 g) all-purpose flour

⅓ cup (65 g) sugar

1 teaspoon baking powder

½ teaspoon salt

SPECIAL EQUIPMENT

Donut pan

1. Preheat the oven to 350°F (175°C). Spray the donut pan with nonstick cooking spray.

2. In a small bowl, combine the egg, milk, butter, and vanilla.

3. In a large bowl, sift together the flour, sugar, baking powder, and salt. Add the wet mixture and mix well, but don't overmix.

4. Spoon or pipe the batter into the donut pan. Bake for 8 to 10 minutes until golden brown. Cool on a baking rack. Note for the polar bear and cub: You won't get donut holes from these pans, so you'll have to sacrifice a full-grown donut and cut it down into round babies.

5. For glazed donuts, go to the next page.

6. For candy dipped donuts, go to the next page.

7. For buttercream frosted donuts, go to page 165.

Glazed

3 cups (375 g) powdered sugar

Pink food coloring (for the flamingo)

Sprinkles (for the flamingo)

1. In a medium bowl, whisk the powdered sugar with ⅓ cup (80 ml) water. Add food coloring until it's the color of your dreams, if making the flamingo.

2. Pour the glaze over the cooled donuts. Add sprinkles, if making the flamingo, while still wet.

3. To add the Best Flamingo Ever or a basic bird shape, go to the next page.

4. To add the Best Polar Bears Ever or basic bears, go to page 168.

Candy Dipped

1 bag (14 to 16 ounces/400 to 455 g) pink or white candy melts

Sprinkles (for the flamingo)

1. Place the candy melts in in a microwave-safe glass bowl. Microwave the candy in 10-second increments, stirring after each, until smooth.

2. Dip one side of the donuts into the melted candy. Allow excess to drip off. Set on a baking rack to harden. Add sprinkles, if making the flamingo, while still wet. Dip the other side of the donuts and the donut holes, if making the polar bear and cub.

3. To add the Best Flamingo Ever or a basic bird shape, go to the next page.

4. To add the Best Polar Bears Ever or basic bears, go to page 168.

Buttercream Frosted

1 cup (2 sticks/225 g) unsalted butter, softened

4 cups (500 g) powdered sugar

2 teaspoons vanilla extract

⅛ teaspoon salt

¼ cup (60 ml) whole milk

Pink food coloring (for the flamingo)

Sprinkles (for the flamingo)

1. In a large bowl, using a mixer, beat the butter until creamy, about 1 minute.

2. Add the powdered sugar 1 cup (125 g) at a time, mixing until well combined.

3. Add the vanilla, salt, and milk, and mix on high until thick and creamy. Add food coloring until desired pink is reached if making the flamingo. If the buttercream is too thin, add more powdered sugar, 1 tablespoon at a time. If the buttercream is too thick, add more milk, 1 tablespoon at a time.

4. Frost the donuts with a layer of buttercream and add the sprinkles if making the flamingo.

5. To add the Best Flamingo Ever or a basic bird shape, see the next column.

6. To add the Best Polar Bears Ever or basic bears, go to page 168.

Best Flamingo Ever

8 ounces (225 g) pink fondant

8 ounces (225 g) white fondant

4 ounces (115 g) black fondant

Yellow, green, blue, and pink food coloring

1. Roll the pink fondant into a thick flamingo head and neck. Use a toothpick or cake wire for extra support. Stick into the donut.

2. Form wings and a tail from the pink fondant. Press them into the donut.

3. Use the white fondant to form eyes and flowers for the head and tray.

4. Use the black fondant to make eyes and a beak.

5. Color fondant brown, blue, and green to make the tray and tropical drinks. You can create the light brown by combining a drop of red and a drop of blue with ten drops of yellow food coloring, and continuing to add the colors in that ratio until you achieve your desired shade.

6. Use water drops to "glue" all the details onto the flamingo. Add details to the feathers and flowers using a paintbrush and toothpicks.

BASIC BIRD SHAPE

8 ounces (225 g) pink fondant

4 ounces (115 g) black fondant

1. Roll the pink fondant into a thick flamingo head and neck. Use a toothpick or cake wire for extra support. Stick into the donut.

2. Form wings and a tail from the pink fondant. Press them into the donut.

3. Use the black fondant to make eyes and beak. Use water drops to "glue" the eyes and beak onto the flamingo head.

POLAR BEAR DONUT AND CUB DONUT HOLE

Nailed It! Holiday! Season 2, Episode 2, "Winter Blunderland"

Makes 10 donuts

DONUT CHOICES

**162
YEAST DOUGH FROM SCRATCH**

PREMADE PIZZA DOUGH
After you've bought a package of pre-made pizza dough at the store, let it come to room temperature and then go straight to "Cutting the Dough"

STORE-BOUGHT DONUTS
Skip to Topping Choices!

BAKING CHOICES

**163
DEEP FRIED**

**163
BAKED**

STORE-BOUGHT DONUTS
Skip to Topping Choices!

TOPPING CHOICES

**164
GLAZED**

**164
CANDY DIPPED**

**165
BUTTERCREAM FROSTED**

LEVEL OF POLAR BEAR DETAIL

**168
BEST POLAR BEARS EVER**

**168
BASIC BEARS**

NONE, THE BEARS ARE HIBERNATING
After you finish your chosen topping method from the previous list:
Ya' done!

Best Polar Bears Ever

8 ounces (225 g) white fondant

4 ounces (115 g) black fondant

4 ounces (115 g) red fondant

Cornstarch

1. Roll the white fondant and form into eyes, ears, noses, paws, and tails (polar bears have short, fluffy, cute ones). Use water drops to "glue" the details onto the donuts and donut holes.

2. Form pupils, noses, and claws from the black fondant. Use water drops to "glue" them onto donuts.

3. Mix little pinches of red and white fondant to make pink fondant. Lighlty dust a flat surface with cornstarch. Roll the pink fondant out to about ⅛ inch (3 mm) thick and cut out shapes for the inside of the ears.

4. Roll out a long strip of white fondant and a long strip of red fondant to about ¼ inch (6 mm) thick. Cut the red fondant into rectangles and attach to the white strip with water drops, leaving spaces between each, to make a striped piece. Wrap around the adult polar bear for a scarf.

5. Add details to faces and paws using a toothpick or a sharp knife.

BASIC BEARS

8 ounces (225 g) white fondant

4 ounces (115 g) black fondant

1. Roll the white fondant and form into eyes, ears, noses, paws, and tails (polar bears have short, fluffy, cute ones). Use water drops to "glue" the details onto the donuts and donut holes.

2. Form pupils and noses from the black fondant. Use water drops to "glue" them onto donuts.

How to Host a

Nailed It!

PARTY

Nailed It! parties are perfect for birthdays, holidays, or whenever you just want to get together with your friends and family, make sweet things, and laugh!

Competition Rules

There are no rules! You can set up your *Nailed It!* party however you'd like. For the seriously competitive, you can set time limits, judge the outcomes, and hand out a glittered chef's hat to the winner. Or you can decide that the ultimate competition is really against your inner critic, and that everyone who tries is a winner. You can have one winner, or many, an award for each category, or a points system. You can have a non-baking judge, have participants judge each other, or do blind judging and taste-testing. The choices are endless!

The *Nailed It!* Award Goes To . . .

If you're looking for suggestions, here are some of our favorite judging categories:

- Tastiest
- Most Beautiful
- Most Creative
- Most Minimalistic
- Most Surprising
- Funniest
- Cleanest Workstation (that one's for you, Jacques!)

Distraction Button Ideas

What's better than someone interrupting your flow with an annoying distraction? A lot of things, but it's super funny to do anyway. With a real button or an imaginary one, you can introduce (by yelling) one-minute challenges at random times when they least expect it (it's funnier that way). A few ideas for your bakers:

- Hop up and down on one leg
- Put one hand behind your back
- Don't use your hands at all
- Sing or hum
- Freeze!
- Close one eye
- Stop and do jumping jacks
- Stand on your tiptoes

HOST A VIRTUAL PARTY

Don't live near Grandma? Your college friends spread out around the country? You can still bake with them by hosting a virtual *Nailed It!* party. You can either livestream your experience or have everyone attempt to make the same dessert and share your spectacular photos and videos afterward.

SWEET SET-UP

For an in-person party, you can provide as much, or as little, for your guests as you desire, depending on what type of baker you are:

Commercial-Size Kitchen Baker

If you've got room and an oven, or ovens, that can handle it, by all means, turn your house into a *Nailed It!* studio and have everyone bake, make, and decorate.

Committed, Slightly Crazy Baker

Pre-make all of the dessert foundations—the cake, the cookies, the donuts, and a mountain of buttercream—for your guests. Have decorating stations set up for them when they arrive.

Committed, but Not to Buttercream, Baker

Pre-bake all of the basics—the cake, the cookies, the donuts—for your guests, but stock up on store-bought frosting, setting out two cans per person, along with decorating supplies.

Community Baker

Ask your guests to bring their own plain cake, cookie, or donut—you'll have everything they need to pretty it up.

Secret Store Shopper Baker

Buy everything from the store: the cake, the cookies, the donuts, the frosting, and the decorations. Large, undecorated sheet cakes can easily be cut up into smaller round or rectangular cakes. Plain cake donuts make a wonderful canvas for getting creative. The fun is in the process anyway!

PARTY-PERFECT RECIPES

CREDITS

Author Heather Maclean is a Princeton grad, celebrity ghostwriter (Mickey Mouse was her first client), and pop culture expert who writes *New York Times* bestselling books about art, science, food, fashion, and reality TV. Visit her at www.heather-maclean.com.

Photos on pages 8–9, 12, 20, 32–33, 54, 108, 114, 127, and 176 by Bruce Finn, © 2020 Magical Elves, LP.

Photos on pages 30, 42, 44, 96, and 98 (Alien Cupcakes, Rocket Ship Cake, and Toy Robot Cake) © 2020 Briana Balducci.

Pages 4–5 and 174–75: oxygen/ Getty Images

Page 6: Vera Livchak/Getty Images

Pages 20, 41, 51, 75, 82, and 118: subjub/ Getty Images

Page 16: tovovan/Getty Images

Pages 4–5, 7, 10–11, 14–15, 20, 41, 50–51, 75, 82, 118: MicrovOne/Getty Images

Front cover (cake stand): ptasha/Getty Images

All other images courtesy of Netflix.

Jacques' Legendary Hot Chocolate recipe on page 134 courtesy of Jacques Torres.

The recipes for Alien Cupcakes (page 30), Rocket Ship Cake (page 42), and Toy Robot Cake (page 96) were developed by Red Velvet NYC for *Nailed It! At Home Experience* virtual events produced by Netflix and Fever.

Red Velvet NYC helps families celebrate life's most precious moments with gourmet DIY baking kits. Established in 2015 by two sisters, the company operates out of Brooklyn, New York. www.redvelvetnyc.com

Fever is the leading entertainment discovery platform with a mission to inspire people through experiences. Fever delivers a curated list of the most exciting events and things to do and see in your city, tailored just for you. www.feverup.com

Editor: Shannon Kelly
Managing Editor: Mike Richards
Designer: Heesang Lee
Production Manager: Rachael Marks

Library of Congress Control Number: 2021932566

ISBN: 978-1-4197-5291-9
eISBN: 978-1-64700-476-7

Printed and bound in the United States
10 9 8 7 6 5 4 3 2 1

Abrams Image books are available at special
discounts when purchased in quantity for
premiums and promotions as well as fundraising
or educational use. Special editions can also be
created to specification. For details, contact
specialsales@abramsbooks.com or the address below.
Abrams Image® is a registered trademark of
Harry N. Abrams, Inc.

ABRAMS The Art of Books
195 Broadway, New York, NY 10007
abramsbooks.com